MW00614615

© 2019, Justin Daab

Author: Justin Daab
Cover & Section Divider Illustration: Tara D., lilbrownbird.com
Graphic Design: Tara D., Tyler Ehrig & Cara Murphy
Photo Illustration: Tyler Ehrig & Cara Murphy
Strategic Nitpicking: Rick Moser

1st Edition: September 2019
ISBN: 978-1-7334165-2-8

www.IAABOOK.com
www.magnani.com
All rights reserved

INNOVATE.

ACTIVATE.

ACCELERATE.

A 30-DAY BOOT CAMP FOR YOUR BUSINESS BRAIN.

CONTENTS

ACKNOWLEDGMENTS

Thanks

First, to my wife and kids who are the constant catalysts for my own introspection, reflection, and desire to learn something new and be a better person every day.

Next, to my family—composed of that which I was born into and that which I married into—who've collectively provided humor, mentorship, shelter, Kashi Mit Bushi (Google it, it's delicious), amazing hand-me-downs, whisky (yes, I use the Scottish spelling), and centuries of collective experiences, which they've shared freely.

And, finally, to everyone I've worked with. I've learned something invaluable from every one of them, with a special shoutout to Rudy Magnani, whose perspectives and mantras formed the foundations of the business I now run and whose words are literally written on the walls of the office, and which directly inspired a few of the following chapters.

Before you commit any hard-earned "me" time to reading this book, I have three confessions:

CONFESSION #1: I don't like most business books.

Generally, I find that most of them present a single kernel of an idea, then repeat it, with slight tweaks, ad nauseam, 20-page chapter after 20-page chapter. Some writers, like Malcolm Gladwell, are amazing at making that structure as entertaining as it is informative. But he's a rare talent. And even with Gladwell, midway through most of his work, admittedly, I find myself weighing the incremental cost of time to read the next chapter against the incremental return of gaining a more nuanced understanding of the topic. To that point, most of these chapters are just a few pages, and each was written to stand up to nonlinear consumption. I have arranged the various topics in what I felt was a logical flow or grouping of ideas. But you'll not be harmed by grazing on any chapter that catches your fancy.

CONFESSION #2: This book contains very few answers.

Points of view? Plenty. Questions you'll need to answer all by yourself? A fair number. My point in compiling the material for this book wasn't to provide answers, but to hopefully help readers reflect on their circumstances from a new perspective. Or, better yet, that the endeavor of scanning these pages embeds some mashup of disparate ideas in their heads so that some synthesis occurs that inevitably reveals an unexpected, new opportunity. Kind of like when you used to stare at those books, filled with stochastic chromatic noise, and if you stare long enough, something akin to the silhouette of a dolphin jumping through a hoop would magically rise up from the background.

CONFESSION #3: If you find this book valuable, you should take all the credit.

But if not, I deserve all the blame. I probably could have numbered this confession "2B." But I like things that appear in groups of three. Anyway, as I mentioned, any real insights, aha's or otherwise-named eureka moments you may experience are because you stopped to reflect on your own circumstances, reexamined a belief or assumption, or did a few back-of-the-envelope calculations that revealed something important. At best, this book can be a catalyst. You are the mastermind. But if nothing within these pages sparks a single moment of exploration, introspection or newfound insight, then shame on me.

YOU'VE BEEN WARNED.

Enjoy.

Short Answer:
No one, specifically.

For any individual concept, idea or strategic musing, your mileage may vary depending on your role, experience, or interest in the topic. If that seems confusing, see the Longer Answer.

Longer Answer:

CEOs

It doesn't matter if you are a small-business owner or running a Fortune 100 company. It's a common occurrence that the day-to-day stresses of running a business can take a toll on your ability to get above it all and think strategically. This book is designed to give you a few minutes a day to reset that part of your brain that welcomes the comfort of business as usual and to restart the process of evaluating strategies and asking, "What if?"

Innovators

An innovator's job is not, as many think, to create new product ideas from thin air. It is to uncover real business opportunities. The ideas and concepts presented in this book were written to give you some added support for finding, evaluating, and launching new ideas. And, most importantly, to evaluate those new ideas in a framework consistent with your business goals and the markets in which you compete.

Strategists

Whether you're looking for a new, strategic approach to solving a business challenge or new approaches for maximizing results from the strategy to which you're already committed, you'll likely find some new ideas to explore here.

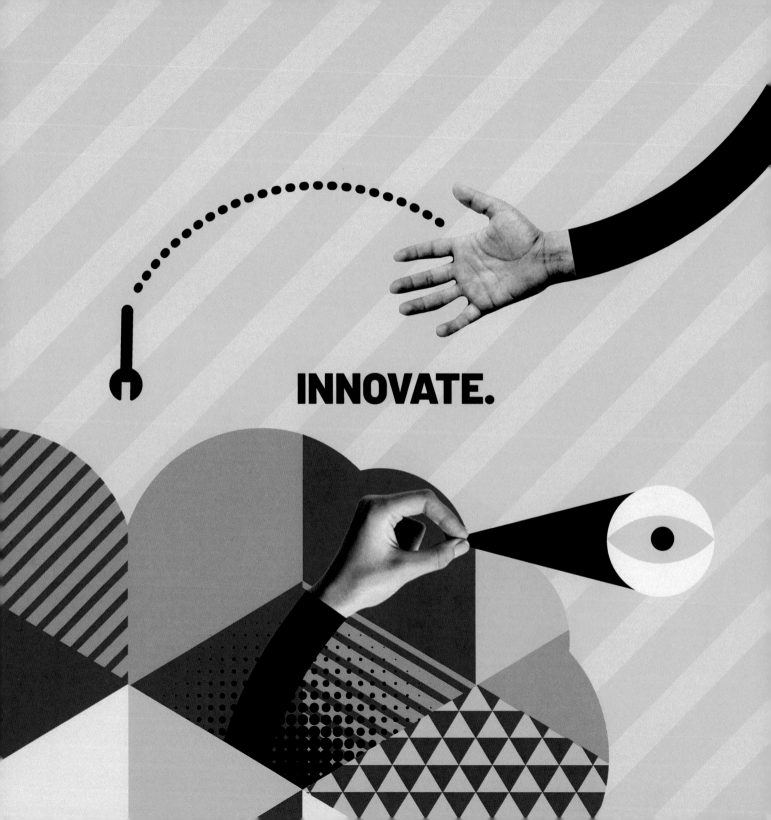

INNOVATE.

"What we did was unprecedented, but what is less well understood is that we had no choice."

–Paul Allen

What will you do?

In business today, competition isn't the most imminent threat—it's complacency. The chapters in this section are less about the creation of ideas than they are about how you shape your attitudes, behaviors and processes in a manner that directs the greatest resources and energy into developing ideas that best serve the customer and the business, alike.

DAY
01

Remember, there's always a "Day 1."

Ready to start innovating? On Day One, ask yourself these five questions.

The myth in popular culture is that innovation is the byproduct of a random spark of inspiration. Lightning strikes. Someone has a eureka moment. The world is forever changed. Sounds quite easy, if mostly unachievable by mere mortals. The truth is that innovation is more often the result of a resolute commitment of time and resources—and a solid innovation process. Committing the resources is simply a matter of availability and will. Creating a strategy can be more complicated. There are, however, some basic questions that every company should ask and answer to begin solidifying a viable innovation strategy that the entire company can rally around.

Q1: What would change the value equation of our industry and our customers?

This is an intentionally broad question, but it is at the root of any successful innovation strategy. For a business, innovation isn't about change for change's sake; it's about taking steps today to secure the greatest share of revenues and profits in the future. And the first step toward gaining a glimpse of what that future looks like is to imagine what the market would look like if you, through your product development efforts, could radically alter the cost structures for the business or its customers, or both. What would the market look like if you could radically alter the product life span? What if you radically changed the scale of your solution? Delivery times?

It's not that you need to answer exactly how you will accomplish this, for now. But you need to decide, as a company, which of those changes could have the greatest impact on the landscape of your industry. Further, whatever you choose to focus on needs to be something you believe is at least somewhat achievable with the application of time and resources.

Q2: How could our business model be disrupted?

One of the best ways to start answering this question is to look at your greatest strengths and the market leader's strengths and start to ask how a new entrant might turn them into a weakness. Ten years ago, few would have predicted that the world's largest taxi company (Uber) would own no taxis, or that the world's largest retailer (Alibaba) would hold no inventory, or that the world's fastest-growing hotelier wouldn't own or manage a single room (Airbnb). But those companies looked at the market leader's greatest strengths and made them weaknesses.

03: What parts of today's business are we willing to sacrifice for tomorrow's innovation?

In his seminal work, "The Innovator's Dilemma," Harvard Business School professor, Clayton Christensen, outlines the ways highly successful companies end up ceding markets to disruptors they easily could have stopped in their tracks had the company been willing to suffer through the opportunity costs of innovation. The point being, sometimes you innovate, and sometimes you have innovation thrust upon you. And it pays to understand in advance how the business could function, thrive or survive with various lines of business or product lines removed.

04: What capital are we willing to invest/risk?

It should come as no surprise, but innovation is rarely inexpensive. In fact, it's usually costly, even comparatively wasteful by normal business investment standards. Where investments in the day-to-day operations are expected to produce standard linear returns, investments in innovation should be thought of more like a venture-capital model—most of them will return nothing, but the home-run ideas deliver 10X returns. It's not math most companies are used to or comfortable with. But failures are as much or more a part of fruitful innovation programs as the successes. A great example of this mentality is Apple. It is widely reported that Apple kills off far more of its R&D projects[1] than it ever sends to market. And that willingness to experiment has obviously served them well.

05: If it ain't broke, why fix it?

It's tempting to think that wildly successful businesses are somehow immune to radical disruption, but none truly are. Traditional relationship businesses could be easily overwhelmed by conversational artificial intelligence (AI). Delivery, distribution, and logistics are in the crosshairs of self-driving vehicles. Accounting, auditing, and title insurance businesses could suddenly find themselves as anachronistic leftovers by blockchain technology. Just as traditional media planning and strategy have succumbed to programmatic models, even formerly technology-resistant creative professions will find themselves pressured by bots that can literally start running the infinite monkeys algorithm until they hit upon the marketing equivalent of Shakespeare. This is not a gloom-and-doom prophecy. It's the call of opportunity resulting from new, disruptive technologies. We just have to keep open minds.

[1] https://www.fastcompany.com/1671718/from-phones-to-tablets-26-apple-designs-that-never-came-to-be

01: What would change the value equation of our industry and our customers?

02: How could our business model be disrupted?

03: What parts of today's business are we willing to sacrifice for tomorrow's innovation?

04: What capital are we willing to invest/risk?

05: If it ain't broke, why fix it?

Download a printable PDF of all notes pages at magnani.com/book

DAY 02

Innovation culture begins with language.

When it comes to creating an innovation culture, you get what you ask for.

On Day One, you started to think about your business in an innovation framework. But how can you increase your chances of everyone in the company thinking with an innovation mindset? I would suggest you do so with a single sentence.

If you want more innovation, change your mission statement.

The Talking Heads may have alluded to this phenomenon most eloquently in the song "Give Me Back My Name." The lyrics read: "There's a word for it, and words don't mean a thing. There's a name for it, and names make all the difference in the world..." The point being, the language we use to describe things, beyond the most basic categorization, can affect our perceptions and, more importantly, the inherent opportunities we see in them.

At no time is this phenomenon more relevant than when crafting your company's mission statement. Far too often, companies fail to see how the language they choose to describe their company, or its mission, can either promote or stifle innovation.

Amazon® is not a retailer.

Amazon states their mission thus: "Our vision is to be Earth's most customer-centric company; to build a place where people can come to find and discover anything they might want to buy online, and endeavors to offer its customers the lowest possible prices." At first blush, you may understand that as meaning they are an online retailer that wants to sell you anything and everything, cheaply. But the more nuanced interpretation, which I believe is correct, is that they quite simply want a cut of every online transaction, period.

To employ an overused phrase from the startup community, Amazon is a platform for facilitating that mission, whether or not Amazon is ultimately the seller. That language leaves them not only open to innovative arrangements like affiliate marketing and contract fulfillment but also to unique partnerships with offerings like Amazon Web Services (AWS).

The perfect example is Netflix[2], which, despite ostensibly being a competitor to Amazon's own Prime Video service, is also one of Amazon's largest AWS customers. You might expect a company to deny its direct competitors access to their foundational content-delivery technology. But denying Netflix access to the service would be in violation of the mission. And, in reality, it's a win-win for all.

Apple® is not a computer company.

"To make a contribution to the world by making tools for the mind that advance humankind." That's how Steve Jobs spoke of the company when he ran it. The statement doesn't focus on any specific hardware. That foresight allowed Apple to expand into more consumer electronics categories beyond its original roots. That expansion, however, highlighted another issue regarding the language with which Apple was describing itself. At the Macworld Expo in 2007, Steve Jobs famously stepped out onto his keynote stage and announced, "The Mac, iPod, Apple TV and iPhone. Only one of those is a computer. So we're changing the name." At that moment, the company ceased being Apple Computer and became simply Apple.

Why did it matter? Would we consumers have purchased fewer iPhones or iPods had the word "computer" been left in the name? Probably not. Jobs understood the power that a simple change in language would have on everyone within the company. To paraphrase, employees would think differently about what constituted a viable opportunity for the business. Since that time, Apple has added services including iTunes, Music, iCloud, the App Store and, most recently, Apple Pay—a few of which are even available through non-Apple-branded hardware.

Is Apple still a hardware company? Of course. But revenue from their services business, for the fourth fiscal quarter of 2018 alone, was reported at a record ~$10 billion—a figure itself large enough to qualify as a Fortune 100 business.

[2] https://aws.amazon.com/solutions/case-studies/netflix

What makes a mission statement innovation-ready?

So, how can you ensure your own mission is at once descriptive, directional and inspirational enough to become the bedrock for an innovation culture? Here are a few questions you may want to ask yourself:

Is the objective aspirational?

Far too often, companies develop mission statements with objectives that are satisfied entirely by their current offering, positioning the job in the minds of employees as "done." For an innovation culture, it's best to always keep the carrot at the end of a moving stick. Instead of asking to be great at what you do, ask for something akin to transformation of the human condition.

Is it broad enough to encompass what's yet to be created?

The point here is that being a company that describes itself as offering "next-generation illumination for the world" provides more opportunity for adapting to new technologies than, say, describing the company as "leaders in incandescent lighting."

Does it glorify the pursuit?

The pursuit of innovation is as much, or more, about taking risks, iterating, failing, and discarding as it is about seizing the reins of the next successful new idea. This suggests the mission should, in kind, elevate the importance of the pursuit as much, or more, than any desired end.

You may ask yourself, "Well, how did I get here?"

It seemed only fitting to end with more lyrics from the Talking Heads. Love them or hate them; they were innovative. And the truth is, the path to innovation is not easily traced through obvious, connected moments of cause and effect. Not everyone in the company will always understand how you got there. But the more breadcrumbs you can leave for everyone along the way—e.g., the company mission statement—the easier it will be for everyone in the company to join in along the journey.

Getting to an innovation-ready mission statement:

Write down your company's current mission statement:

In what ways is your current mission statement aspirational, broad, or energizing?
Or, in what ways is it not?

What, if any, impending market shifts or changes might compromise the value of your current mission statement?

List five ways your company helps people that do not mention your specific products or services:

Draft three unique innovation-ready mission statements.

Download a printable PDF of all notes pages at magnani.com/book

DAY 03

Learn to see with new eyes.

Innovate. Activate. Accelerate.

On inattentional blindness and disruption hunting.

There is a great YouTube video that begins by asking the viewer to watch a group of casual basketball players and count how many times they pass the basketball between themselves. Spoiler alert: This video is not about your knowledge of basketball or counting skills. And if you haven't seen it, go here:

Okay, welcome back. The point of bringing this video up here is that disruption opportunities are like the gorilla. Once you know to look for them, you can't believe you missed them earlier.

3 https://youtu.be/vJG698U2Mvo

Disruption follows patterns anyone can track.

As we mentioned earlier, the idea often propagated by startup founders and venture capitalists is that innovation and disruption are the results of magical inspiration. But the truth is, it's more likely that disruptive market entrants simply examined the structure of the industry or market and saw some telltale signs that anyone could see—if they knew where to look.

Culturally, when thinking or speaking about disruption, we place a lot of emphasis on the act of creation. But that is the second step—the first is spotting the opportunity. For Day Three, I'm going to outline just a few of the signs any disruption hunter should look for when deciding upon which industry to set his or her sights. Any one of these characteristics may be reason enough to start building a disruptive solution, but if you see more than one of these signs, there is a greater chance you have found vulnerable prey.

Thar be whales.

A classic sign that an industry is ripe for disruption is that it's dominated by a small number of massive competitors. Usually, when markets consolidate, the few main players at the top of the food chain have little incentive to take risks and alter the status quo. And the more settled the industry, the more the incumbents have to lose, effectively slowing their ability to react to disruption without sacrificing revenues, or, at least, margin.

Most of us watched the entertainment industry lose control of distribution to streaming upstarts because they refused to give up analog dollars chasing digital dimes. Most folks also watched the hospitality industry refuse to unbundle the physical plant from the service offering and let Airbnb become the de facto travel behavior of an emerging generation. But a few seasoned disruption hunters saw the signs, and, as a result, forever changed the way we listen to music or book travel accommodations.

Tin cans and string.

It should be obvious, but if the industry has cruised for decades atop outdated technology, there's a good chance disrupting that industry is a real possibility. It's not a given, however, that simply deploying alternative technology wins the day. The critical question is how much customer value can be added or extracted by deploying an alternative technology platform?

Whether it was in the first dot-com craze of the late 1990s or the "there's an app for that" hysteria from just a few years back, it's not new technology platforms that provide a material disruptive advantage but it's how those platforms can alter the user experience in a meaningful way.

Uber didn't succeed because of its mobile app—it succeeded because it leveraged emerging technologies to systematically address a number of long-standing user experience issues, for passengers and drivers alike. It ultimately reduced uncertainty of rider/driver availability, route, cost, and gratuity, to name a few.

It's a relationship business.

As a disruptive innovator, the moment anyone tells you technology cannot replace a relationship sell, you should at least entertain the idea of proving them wrong. By nature, industries rely on relationships when there's a lack of transparency or arcane complexity inherent in the transaction.

But those are precisely the kinds of industries we've seen disrupted successfully. Lemonade simplified the process of obtaining renters insurance. Just point your mobile device at the property you want to insure— no agent or broker necessary. Intuit® disintermediated mortgage brokers and launched Rocket Mortgage®, allowing consumers to get preapproved for a home loan in hours instead of days.

The lesson here is, while an underlying transaction might have inherent complexity, who bears the burden of that complexity makes all the difference from a customer experience standpoint. Traditionally, intermediaries like agents and brokers shouldered the burden for the end customer, e.g., navigating arcane application processes that service providers saw no reason to simplify. But disruptive entrants realized if they shifted the burden of complexity behind internal processes and controls, they could provide consumers a level of simplicity even greater than the handholding provided by a broker or agent.

Trust is outsourced.

Trust management generally falls into a few basic categories: identity, provenance and security. Identity, meaning you (as a person or piece of data) are who you purport to be in the context of this interaction or transaction. Provenance, meaning you (as a person or piece of data) are from where you say you are from. Security, meaning you (as a person or piece of data) are protected from theft, duplication or alteration.

Historically, providing some form of trust management service meant amassing increasingly large databases of past transactions against which to verify the next transaction. But, as we've seen through recent high-profile data breaches like that which occurred at Equifax®, centralization of this kind of information merely creates a virtual honey pot of opportunity for hackers—both independent and state-sponsored.

We've mentioned before that a hallmark of disruption is turning the incumbents' greatest strengths into weaknesses. Industries that rely on third-party centralized honey pots of consumer data for trust management are ripe for disruption. New entrants employing recent technological advances like cryptography (e.g., blockchain, bitcoin, et al.) or machine learning (e.g., Palantir) will most surely turn that equation inside out.

A necessary evil.

When the majority of consumers of an entrenched industry view their interactions with or within that industry negatively, the barriers preventing entrance of a disruptive competitor are very low. Any new entrant need only focus on minimizing switching costs, both financial and temporal, and a decent contingent of customers will gladly give any new solution a try. And the longer the industry has maintained its unfavorably viewed practices, the lower that barrier becomes.

Happy hunting.

This is by no means a definitive guide, but if you can start viewing individual industries and markets through these lenses, opportunities for innovation or disruption will surely come into focus. Remember, technologies don't disrupt industries or markets—they enable people with smart visions to make them a reality.

Can you identify and list out any industries (including your own) that exemplify any of these target behaviors?

When you think about those industries, what disruptive solutions come to mind?

How would a disruptive entrant into your market view your business through these lenses?

Download a printable PDF of all notes pages at magnani.com/book

DAY 04

Think like a customer from another planet.

Looking for a path to growth?
Change your perspective.

Whether simply beginning to map out long-term product or technology road maps, examining areas of exploration or innovation, analyzing channel strategy, or simply wanting more from existing customers, most companies focus on accelerating or augmenting existing behaviors. But, at some point, that approach delivers diminishing returns. Or, worse, a disruptive competitor. To that end, every company seeking business growth would be well served by asking:

What are my customers really buying?

The first big mistake most companies make is believing their customers are buying a thing—a specific product or service. Meaning, your basic widget manufacturer thinks they're satisfying a consumer's desire to own a widget. That frame of mind works well enough in most cases. You can survey the market fairly efficiently and determine the total current market for widgets. You can do a bit of Google searching and know how many other widget manufacturers are out there. And, finally, you can do a bit of math and quickly determine whether you're getting more or less of your reasonably fair share of the market. The problem with that perspective is that it tends to limit the range of growth ideas to those defined by their widgetness: Better widgets. Bigger widgets. Cheaper widgets.

Harvard Business School's (HBS's) Clayton Christensen views consumer transactions from a different perspective. In his book "Competing Against Luck," Christensen posits products are not purchased but rather "hired" by the customer to do a specific job. And if a company can unravel the relationship, it gives them more and better avenues along which to innovate—creating better candidates for the available job.

One example he cites in his classes at HBS is that of a milkshake company[4] that hired Christensen and his team to help boost sales. Through a series of post-purchase interviews with customers at the milkshake purveyor's retail outlets, Christensen was able to determine that, for most buyers, the job the milkshake was hired for wasn't sustenance or even pleasure, per se, but a distraction during a long commute home. That the physical challenge of pulling a thick shake through a straw was the perfect distraction to help make the long drive more tolerable.

[4] https://hbswk.hbs.edu/item/clay-christensens-milkshake-marketing

The company used that insight to create a new line of shakes, both thicker, to last longer, and more engaging through the addition of fruit chunks and other bits, to deliver additional joy and keep drivers more "shake engaged." Changing perspective and understanding what their customers were buying—entertainment and distraction—opened new avenues for product innovation and growth.

Does my business really have to work this way?

The second big mistake many make is assuming the way you're currently doing business is the right way and that the logical path to follow leads is doing more of it. As soon as you resign yourself to a specific channel strategy, technology platform, distribution model, et al., you close yourself off to potential opportunities and open opportunities for new market entrants.

Case in point: Casper mattresses. Prior to Casper, the mattress retail experience adhered to a few fairly strict experience guidelines. First, the buyer had to be able to try out the mattress in a retail showroom before purchase—usually under the watchful eye of a sales associate. A mattress was too large a purchase to make blindly. Adding to that risk was guideline number two—retailers would do just about anything not to have to take returns on mattresses. And, three, selling mattresses direct, online, wouldn't be financially viable due to the shipping costs.

In 2014, Casper turned literally every aspect of the purchasing process upside down. The mattresses ship to a customer's doorstep, highly compressed in a box of only 19"x19"x41"—keeping shipping reasonable. Customers are free to sleep on the mattress in their own home for 100 nights. If they return it, Casper picks it up and donates the mattress to a local charity. Truly a disruptive entrant. An article from Fortune[5] nicely encapsulates the dangers of the incumbent being too wedded to their model:

"At first, big mattress companies dismissed the 'bed-in-a-box' trend as a niche phenomenon, hardly worth acknowledging; but that was before the startups grabbed 9% of U.S. market share. In August 2016, Sealy® launched Cocoon by Sealy, a bed-in-a-box brand boasting minimalist fonts, an uncluttered scrolling webpage, and a price point half that of Casper's. 'It's been a delayed reaction, but now they all have bed-in-a-box products,' says Seth Basham, senior vice president of equity research at Wedbush Securities. As for Casper, Basham adds, 'They've already got a foothold. Now it's a matter of how big they'll grow.'"

[5] http://fortune.com/2017/08/23/casper-mattress-philip-krim/

In what way are you failing customers?

Sometimes the toughest act for a company, or an entire industry, is to take an honest look in the mirror and document its flaws. That means really taking the time to understand the end-to-end customer experience and cataloguing every point of friction, pain or frustration. Then, looking at those points and asking, "If these flaws, no matter how insignificant they may seem, were critical enough to put me out of business tomorrow, how would I remedy them and how much effort would I be willing to put forth doing so?" History has shown US market entrants who address issues that companies imagined were trivial can radically alter the competitive landscape. Sometimes that thing can be as small as an emoji.

Starting in 2010, Domino's® Pizza started looking in the mirror and being honest about what it saw, or, rather, tasted. It admitted that its pizza was, shall we say, "less than tasty." So, their first action was to admit it to themselves and to the world through their advertising. The second was, obviously, to reformulate. Setting aside whether you subjectively agree that the outcome of that reformulation was an improvement, objectively the market began to take notice.

Continuing the examination, Domino's started to look at every aspect of the ordering experience, leading ultimately to what I would say is the most frictionless ordering experience in their industry: the emoji order. Once you are in their system, your mobile number registered, the only thing between you and a fresh, hot, delivered pizza is one texted pizza emoji.

Was ordering a pizza via a phone call, the web, or a mobile app really a "fail?" Easy enough, right? Maybe. But given the number of pizzas ordered by those under the influence of any number of intoxicating substances every year, something as simple as an emoji just might substantially increase their chances of completing that order successfully. And it's a pretty entertaining experience for everyone else, too.

And addressing those seemingly minor "fails" has had a major positive impact on their stock price.

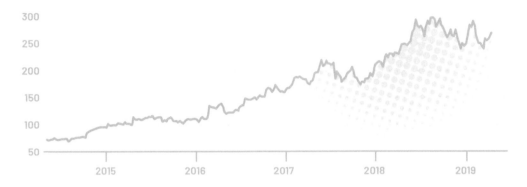

It's never easy to see past our experiences or biases.

But when a company can be deliberate about the process of self-examination and inquiry, and take on the perspective of an observer from another planet, opportunities reveal themselves.

What are my customers really buying? (Status? Time? Convenience? Savings?)

Does my business really have to work this way? (How else could we serve our best and worst customers)?

In what ways are we failing our best customers? (What tradeoffs/costs are they accepting for transacting with us?)

Download a printable PDF of all notes pages at magnani.com/book

DAY 05

Pick the right path.

So, we can all agree, disruption isn't magic.

Hopefully, we've dispelled the popular mythology that nobody sees disruption coming. Or, that disruptive businesses, like unicorns, appear as if by magic, to upend the status quo. Or that the disruptors are mad wizards who somehow see the future no one else could have. And, hopefully, by Day Five here, you're inclined to agree that disruptors actually follow a very linear thought process, and those companies being disrupted are more victims of their current successes than they are caught sleeping at the wheel.

Even the best companies are vulnerable.

More than half of the companies listed in the Fortune 500 in 2000 have since been removed—dethroned by a more technologically savvy disruptor. And, it's predicted that, between now and 2025, half again will have succumbed to a similar fate.

There is a basic development trajectory of disruptive innovation any company can recognize, but there are also myriad logical reasons why successful companies fail to act when smaller, even less well-funded, disruptors enter the scene. But how do you know you're not following the "dinosaur's" path today in your own industry— great at the game you're playing but not realizing the game itself is about to change? The only way to know is to start down the path.

Three Proven Paths to Disruptive Innovation:

01. Launch tomorrow's market offering, today.

Is your target segment a growing or shrinking demographic? Are there macroeconomic trends that will have any major impact on the size of your current markets? Are there any shifting generational or social norms that could affect perceptions of your brand or your offering?

Choosing which trends might materially affect your markets one day is an art form, to be sure. But the idea here is to scour secondary research sources and glean from that data the most relevant bits to help model a snapshot of your market at some specific point in the future—two years, five years— when you believe those trends will converge to a tipping point for the current market.

For a relevant example, we can look at the hospitality industry. In it, there is any number of examples of companies using this type of analysis to shift their offering to meet future demand. Case in point, while Generation X may currently represent the largest segment of business travelers, many of the leading hoteliers have focused their innovation teams on changing their room and common-space designs to address the impending market dominance of millennial business travelers.

Watch a Gen-X-aged business traveler enter a recently renovated room at a Marriott, and you'll likely see them looking all around the room for a desk that isn't there. Watch a millennial business traveler enter the same room, and they'll sit on the bed and pull out their laptop without a second glance for a desk they'd likely never use anyway. Common areas are being similarly transformed. Where once hotels created separate lobby, work, and dining areas with nationally recognized eateries, current renovations are delivering integrated common rooms and unique culinary options derived from local influences.

02. Expose your industry's deepest, darkest secret.

In most industries, there's some fact about the standard business model that no one really wants to talk about because, though it may be inconvenient for the customer, it drives significant revenue. Take, for example, the insurance industry. Everyone in the industry would tell you that it is, by necessity, a relationship business. To get insured properly, you need a guy or gal in the business who knows the business; because every customer is unique, getting the best premium is math-intensive, and the process is too arcane for the issuance of a policy to happen any other way.

On top of that, once you were insured, having a claim processed and (hopefully) paid was often a weeks-long undertaking. Customer complaints about that extended timespan were met with explanations that processing a claim required multiple checks and balances and a great deal of necessary paperwork.

Though, as evidenced by previously mentioned insurance industry upstart Lemonade, it is likely more accurate to say the deepest, darkest secret of the insurance industry was its penchant for obfuscation. Despite the industry's claims, the truth was that most customers fell into common risk profiles and adding obfuscation and complexity in how premiums were calculated reduced price comparison opportunities. On top of that, claim delays were likely more about earning a greater amount of interest on cash reserves than it was about extensive investigations.

Lemonade began providing renters and home insurance for urban dwellers through an AI-fueled mobile app, in a process that takes less than two minutes. And claims processing and payment? Three minutes. Further, instead of paying annually, Lemonade customers can "subscribe" to their coverage on a monthly basis.

The innovation here doesn't appear to have stemmed from a single aha moment. It seems to be the product of a systematic, cumulative uncovering of all of the ways the insurance industry intentionally complicates the offering to protect existing revenue streams.

03. Create a future where your industry's greatest strength is a weakness.

This has demonstrably been the most fruitful path to success for disruptive businesses in the past decade. Just look at Alibaba™, Uber, or Airbnb®. Prior to Alibaba, retailers professed their strength by touting the depth and scale of their inventory. Nothing could compare to "Everything, in stock!" Alibaba became the largest retailer in the world expressly by creating a business model where they carry no inventory at all. Love them or hate them, the same approach was quite successfully taken by Uber. They have grown to be the world's largest taxi company, expanding rapidly in more than 80 countries, and they own no taxis. Airbnb? The fastest-growing hotelier in the world because they explicitly own no property. Ironically, the most current example of this strategy might be Amazon's recent push to open physical storefronts—differentiating themselves from increasing online retail competition by creating enhanced opportunities for more personal interactions as well as faster local deliveries.

Innovators understand that if you can envision a way to threaten the value of an industry's greatest asset, the industry will instinctively apply resources to protect that asset, temporarily giving the innovator plenty of runway upon which to gather momentum.

Pick a path. Now act like, or fund, a startup.

Technology, machine learning, and automation are lowering barriers to entry in every industry. Emerging generations expect better solutions. Disruption is imminent. If you're charged with improving the long-term competitiveness of your business, you have two main choices: Disrupt, or be disrupted. The point here is that it doesn't take a massive spark of genius to spot the next disruptive opportunity. It only takes commitment to taking the path.

How will your industry look different in five years?

_____
_____
_____
_____
_____
_____
_____
_____

What is your industry's deepest, darkest secret?

_____
_____
_____
_____
_____
_____
_____
_____

What is the market leader's greatest strength, and how can that be used against them?

_____
_____
_____
_____
_____
_____
_____
_____

Download a printable PDF of all notes pages at magnani.com/book

DAY 06

Rig the odds in your favor.

In innovation, there's no silver bullet. It's silver buckshot.

The writing is on the wall. Literally. If you walk into the breakroom/lunchroom/disco/'80s arcade at Magnani, you'll see the title phrase of this post permanently (well, at least as permanent as vinyl transfer letters can be) scribed on the wall. "There's no silver bullet. It's silver buckshot." It was a favorite phrase of the firm's founder, Rudy Magnani. At the time he said it, Rudy was referring to his philosophy on the successful practice of integrated marketing—but the sentiment applies as well to how continuous innovation is necessary for continuing success.

The odds of any one innovation succeeding are dismal.

The common wisdom is that 9 out of 10 innovations fail. And by fail, we mean someone or some entity believed in the idea enough initially to apply money, human capital or both to make it work, and they simply couldn't sustain the endeavor. That applies both to standalone companies and major projects within existing enterprises. So, with odds like that, why bother? Simply put, a successful innovation can easily return more than 10X its initial investment capital.

The odds of some innovations succeeding are pretty good.

The smartest companies approach innovation investing like venture capitalists. VCs invest in a lot of ideas. They form little to no emotional attachment to any single idea. They write off obvious underperformers early. They ignore the breakout successes—they take care of themselves. And they spend the bulk of their efforts trying to maximize the middling investments that could go either way. One reason for this approach is that on the extreme ends of the success curve, obvious market forces prevail. But, in the middle is where you find the "better than market" return opportunities. There, execution can make a difference.

How venture capitalists expect their portfolios to perform:

	BAD	ALIVE	OKAY	GOOD	GREAT	TOTAL
HIGH RISK	$200	$400	$200	$100	$100	$1,000
PAYOUT YEAR 5	0	1x	5x	10x	20x	—
GROSS RETURN	$0	$400	$1,000	$1,000	$2,000	$4,400
NET RETURN	-$200	$0	$800	$900	$1,900	$3,400

Source: https://hbr.org/1998/11/how-venture-capital-works

It takes balls—and lots of them.

Think of it like the classic pinboard and steel ball demonstration museums use to illustrate a normal distribution. You drop a ball down the pinboard. It bounces from pin to pin, succumbing to the forces of gravity and chaotic uncertainty, eventually landing at some point along the bottom of the board.

Galton Board 500
https://www.youtube.com/watch?v=EMK5WPRjGgA

If you invest in a single ball drop, hoping it will land at the far right of the board, your odds of success are terrible. Chaos reigns supreme. But with a large number of drops, no amount of tinkering with the pins could stop some of the steel balls from bouncing to the far ends of the display. You can safely predict a normal distribution of results—from failures to breakout stars.

An experienced tinkerer could, however, strategically bend a few pins and skew the distribution to shift the aggregate distribution curve toward one end or the other. Your innovation efforts should focus on creating, shepherding and tinkering with a large enough portfolio of ideas that randomness and market chaos pose only small threats to your overall success.

In the end, the game is rigged—if you do it right.

The romantic notion of innovation is that it is spawned from a single lightning bolt of inspiration. And that can happen. But building a long-term innovation capability within an organization is usually better served by a systematic approach to generating the proverbial storm front, increasing the chances of lightning striking again and again.

If you had 20% of your EBITDA to invest in R&D or innovation (come on, dream),
how would you spend it?

List all of the innovation or development projects currently underway within your organization:

Map those projects on the following grid.

HIGH RISK

LOW REWARD

HIGH REWARD

LOW RISK

If you were forced to cancel 25% of those projects, but not your overall budget, what would you cut and where would you reallocate the funds?

Download a printable PDF of all notes pages at magnani.com/book

DAY 07

Play the long game.

It usually takes years to be an overnight success.

How many of Edison's more than 1,000 inventions can you name? There's the electric lightbulb, the phonograph, the motion picture camera ... and all the others. And that's the point. For every notable invention Edison patented, there were dozens more along the lines of his electric pen[6].

This is not meant to be some kind of dig on Thomas Edison. To the contrary, it's meant to once again disavow our collective perception of the innovation process as the result of instantaneous magic—lightbulbs appearing over someone's head, or Newton's instant perception of gravity as an apple fell from a tree, etc. The design for a working electric light did not appear above Edison's head. It emerged from iteration and tenacity. According to an entry in Rutgers University's "The Edison Papers,"[7] in an 1890 interview in Harper's monthly magazine, Edison was quoted as saying:

"I speak without exaggeration when I say that I have constructed three thousand different theories in connection with the electric light, each one of them reasonable and apparently to be true. Yet only in two cases did my experiments prove the truth of my theory."

The point is that one should never expect innovation to be efficient. By nature, you're heading into uncharted territory. Which brings up the next truth to consider.

In his book "The Outliers," Malcolm Gladwell outlines what I'll paraphrase as his 10,000-hours-to-greatness theory. In it, he posits that those special few who achieve greatness do so less from any natural abilities than from dedicating the better part of a decade practicing and honing their craft.

Innovators are normally constrained by the same calculus. Much like Edison, it took James Dyson 15 years and more than 5,000 prototypes to make a proper bagless vacuum.[8] Sure, he's worth $5 billion now. But getting there nearly bankrupted him early on.

Further, when you begin to examine how long it takes[9] for even the most important products to reach any sort of critical mass of adoption within the marketplace, innovation is clearly a game for those comfortable taking the long view.

[6] http://electricpen.org/
[7] http://edison.rutgers.edu/
[8] https://www.inc.com/ilan-mochari/vacuum-innovation.html
[9] https://hbr.org/2013/11/the-pace-of-technology-adoption-is-speeding-up

You have to build failure into any success model.

Thinking back to the venture capitalists' very rough rule of thumb from the previous chapter, among all of the investments they make, if they can stick to that schedule, failures and all, they are generally making better-than-average returns on the total portfolio. Granted, it's not a sound strategy for any normal investor looking for someplace safe to slowly grow their money over time, but it's perfect if your investments are collectively high-risk/high-reward endeavors. And if your innovation program doesn't fit that description, you're probably not actually innovating.

So, how can you realize better-than-average returns on your innovation efforts over the long haul?

Despite all of this discussion of failure and risk, innovation programs are not simply a drawn-out game of dice. Even within the innovation numbers game, there are proven ways to increase your chances of success, besides simply having the tenacity to ride out the failed iterations along the way.

01. Define your area(s) of focus.

Try to determine what aspect(s) of your industry or category offer(s) the greatest opportunity for disruptive innovation. Is it in product cost? Performance? Service model?

02. Focus your team.

Create a dedicated innovation group. Make sure they're charged with creating new innovation projects, as well as shepherding them—both the successes and the failures—through to completion. That could mean dedicated R&D staff, dedicated project teams, or at least dedicated project leaders who can manage individual resources on an ad hoc basis to move ideas from inspiration to commercialization. A great example is how Steve Jobs created a self-contained team when creating the Macintosh, even going as far as to move them to a separate building with a pirate flag atop it.

03. Know your end user.

This may be the most important safeguard of success. Great innovation is about solving for real human needs and challenges. When component bells and whistles drop in price, should you add more bells and whistles or create a cheaper bell-and-whistle delivery system? Unless you know what truly matters to your existing and potential users, you have no reasonable way to determine which path offers the greatest chance for success. In other words, delve into the emotional requirements of your customers, present and future.

Everyone rolls the dice. But smart innovators take the time to figure out where to shave off a corner here and there to make the numbers come up in their favor more often.

What areas of innovation, R&D or exploration offer the greatest opportunities for disruptive innovation?

Who in the organization is dedicated to ensuring those areas are well supported and/or explored?

If you spent 5% of EBITDA to better understand your customers, on what areas of understanding would you invest?

Download a printable PDF of all notes pages at magnani.com/book

DAY 08

Put your big idea on trial.

The big idea.

It can happen at any point in a company's life cycle. You think that you should enter additional markets with your existing enterprise, create a new company to take advantage of another market, or launch an idea into a business that can create an entirely new market from scratch. Whether it's a startup or global enterprise, the question immediately following the big idea should always be "How big is the opportunity, really?" Well, actually, the answer to that is more easily parsed into five constituent questions, each of which has the potential to make or to break when it comes to real-world outcomes.

Q1: What problem are you trying to solve?

All too often, the rationale for launching a new venture is founded on the notion that something is possible, regardless of whether that thing (product or service) actually solves for some underserved human need. Take Uber, for example. While it may be tempting to say that the success of Uber was based on the fact that they created an app for ride-sharing, there really wasn't a preexisting pervasive problem one could define as "not having an app for that."

The problems Uber solved were far more fundamentally human. The first, I'll posit, was that anyone who has tried to hail a cab on a downtown street, anywhere near rush hour, has felt at least a twinge of humiliation as they flailed their arms about only to be passed by multiple cabs that already contained passengers. Uber solved for that.

The second issue with the traditional cab experience that caused most people discomfort was that moment of performing either the financial or moral calculus of determining a proper tip as they're trying to exit a cab. Using Uber solved for this as well (even though, until recently, that tip didn't actually go to the driver).

And, in hindsight, Uber bridged a divide across income strata within the society. There were people who wanted and could afford to be driven. And there were people willing to drive them for a nominal fee. Uber facilitated connecting these two parties while simultaneously removing any potentially uncomfortable acknowledgment of each other's financial status.

The point of this is simply that before your company invests in delivering a new product or service, you should be able to answer how it will satisfy a real human need (see: Maslow), and, hopefully, how it does that better than existing, cheaper, or more convenient alternatives.

Q2: How many potential customers have this problem?

While the previous question required soul-searching speculation, properly understanding the size of your target segment requires research, cold hard math, and a little informed guesswork. First, assuming you have a hypothesis of the type of person to whom your new venture might appeal, you'll want to know how many of those folks exist in your trading area, and also understand the size of the market for existing alternatives. You can find that information in a number of ways.

In the US, you might consult the US Bureau of Labor Statistics, US census data, or purchase any number of research reports available through sources like Mintel, or Nielsen. Ultimately, it comes down to a function of how many people fit the demographic or professional profile you've outlined for your target, adjusted by what percentage of them are currently using an existing solution.

Q3: How many of those customers are willing to pay to solve it, and how much?

Here, the question is, really, of those potential customers in your assumed target, "How likely are they to be attracted to and commit to adopting or switching to your proposed new solution?" The uncovering of this could take on a number of forms. Qualitative research, like focus groups, or quantitative surveys, could be used to get a rough estimate of potential desire.

You could probe for price elasticity information among those who claim interest. In the end, the conservative interpretation of any of this kind of research would incorporate some form of discounting—meaning more people will claim interest and intent than you can count on actually converting.

Q4: How often will they need to solve the problem?

So, if you know roughly how many people might want to pay for your new product or service, and how much they may be willing to pay, the next logical data point when determining the real magnitude of opportunity is how often do they need it? Is it a one-off purchase? A subscription? Seasonal? Annual?

Q5: How protectable/defensible is it?

In a perfectly competitive market, every player gets an equal share and profit margins quickly drop to zero. No one should enter that kind of market. So, the question anyone embarking on a potential game-changing venture should ask themselves is, what is the barrier of entry for your competitors? Do you have protectable intellectual property? Do you have an operational or cost advantage that is not easily replicated?

In his book "Zero to One, Notes on Startups and How to Build the Future," venture capitalist Peter Thiel frames this question around the idea of whether your insight or I.P. is capable of effectively creating a monopoly. And, more importantly, can you defend that monopoly long enough to recoup R&D and return a high multiple for investors before any real margin-eroding competition takes root?

And that's just stage one.

Obviously, this is by no means a complete list of the outstanding questions facing any new venture. They are simply a start to providing the intellectual checks and balances to the emotional excitement of a new business idea. You still have questions about product and/or experience design, staffing, KPIs, branding, positioning, messaging, media, and distribution strategy to answer, just to name a few. But those are issues for another day.

What problem are you trying to solve?

How many potential customers have this problem?

How many of those customers are willing to pay to solve it, and how much?

How often will they need to solve the problem?

_____

_____

_____

_____

_____

_____

_____

_____

How protectable/defensible is your solution?

_____

_____

_____

_____

_____

_____

_____

_____

_____

Download a printable PDF of all notes pages at magnani.com/book

DAY 09

Always do the math.

Back to the numbers:
How to evaluate growth opportunities.

In the more than 30 years our firm has existed, we've never had a client come to us and reveal that they had unlimited time and unlimited funds to apply to their growth challenges. When developing a strategic road map, each and every one had to weigh the opportunities and opportunity costs of every decision and prioritize those efforts and investments that would yield the greatest net returns to the business.

As one undergoes the strategic-planning process, understanding what potential opportunity may result from any strategic priority will undoubtedly require a mix of assumption and intuition, and, more importantly, basic quantitative analysis.

So, for Day Nine, we wanted to outline a couple of basic but powerful formulas and processes to assist you in some of the most common areas of inquiry: market sizing and budget prioritization.

In other words, "How big is the opportunity, overall?" and "How should budget dollars be allocated to ensure maximum average returns?"

Part 1—How to calculate potential market size.

In the last chapter, we recommended answering the question "How many of those customers are willing to pay to solve this problem, and how much?" So, here, we're going to go over what that math might look like. Estimating the size of any new market is a mixture of art (the assumptions you're making) and science (the hard evidence you have to quantify the validity of each assumption). Now, there are plenty of folks willing to stake their reputations and their businesses on a purely art-based approach—you could say relying on emotional confidence versus statistical confidence—but the following formulas deliver far more reliable results if you back up your input variables with actual research data. So, what are the variables that go into your formula?

Total Population (P):

This simply corresponds to the total population in your trading area. That could be local, regional, national or global. P = Total Geographical Population

Percentage of Target Customers (PTC):

The percentage of the total population that fits the target segments most likely to be active customers.

Average Transaction Quantity (Q):

The average quantity purchased by a single user at a time.

Frequency of Purchase (F):

How many times the product or service is purchased in the most relevant period of time (annually/quarterly, etc.).

Price of Product (R):

What the expected revenue generated is per transaction.

Market Size (MS) Formula:

(Get ready, this is the math part) $MS = P * PTC * F * R$

An Example:

Since the advent of bike-share programs around the country, articles keep popping up about the need for single-use or limited-use helmets. So, let's say you've just invented a new recyclable engineered paper bicycle helmet for bike-share usage. And you want to launch it in a test market, like Chicago. In 2017, Divvy claimed more than 37,000 members, so, in this example, we can use that for P.

$$P = 37,000$$

But all 37,000 will not be in the market for our new helmet. How many will be? This is where it would behoove you to do some actual quantitative research (the science) among Divvy members to determine levels of need and interest. Let's say we conducted a quantitative online survey with a representative sample (300) Divvy members that indicated 50% of them already own their own traditional bike helmets. Of the remaining 50%, half again of those will never wear a helmet. So, we are left with 25% of the original population that do not own a helmet and are not opposed to using them. But only half of those (the remaining 12.5%) said they would be interested in purchasing your helmet. So, in the end:

$$PTC = .125 \text{ (or 12.5\%)}$$

Each consumer would generally only purchase one helmet at a time, so:

$$Q = 1$$

But the helmets only last about four weeks before the paper breaks down, and most Divvy members only bike 3.5 months out of the year. Discounting for the fact that most people will not be diligent about replacing the helmets in a timely fashion, let's put the frequency of purchase at 2.5 per year.

$$F = 2.5$$

And, finally, you've designed the helmet to sell for about $10, so:

$$R = 10$$

So, let's plug those into the formula!

$$MS = P * PTC * F * R$$

Market size (MS) = 37,000 * .125 * 1 * 2.5 * 10

-or- MS = $115,625

After going through those calculations, you realize there's a reason the idea of single-use helmets comes up every year, yet no one is developing single-use helmets.

Part 2—How to prioritize marketing budgets for growth.

Every marketer faces similar challenges when it comes to budget prioritization. It always comes down to determining against which products or services do you spend what portion of the budget. And, always, the calculus centers on ultimately realizing the greatest returns for every dollar spent. Surprisingly, even though this is an ongoing concern, many marketers rely more on gut intuition than quantitative reasoning.

To add a little more quantitative reasoning into the mix, we'll introduce you to another simple calculation (courtesy of McKinsey & Co) called the customer growth index (CGI). It's an interesting way to understand the correlation between initial consideration and growth potential.

Simply put, to arrive at the CGI, you take the percent of time your brand is a member of your customers' initial consideration set, then divide that by your brand's current market share, and, finally, multiply that result by 100 to create an index. The closer to 100, the greater the brand's ability to keep up with the pace of growth in the market as a whole.

$$CGI = \% \text{ consideration} * \% \text{ market share} * 100$$

McKinsey uses this for looking at overall brand, but we think it can be a useful tool if you know the same inputs within each of your product categories. Let's say Nike was evaluating marketing budget allocations for shoes, apparel and tech wearables. By calculating the Nike CGI for each product category, they would have a better indication of the brand health in each, and which are more or less likely to experience growth for each marketing dollar applied. It's not the end-all determination of which categories should get what budgets, but it's a strong signal of momentum that should be taken into consideration.

Lasting success is calculated.

Marketing is always a blend of art and science. No matter what the size of the market opportunity or propensity for growth, we all need to deliver memorable, motivational experiences for our customers. In the end, these formulas can simply help provide an additional objective sense of perspective in the planning process.

Write down a new market that looks attractive to you:

_____

_____

_____

_____

_____

_____

_____

_____

Work through the two calculations below.

MS = P * PTC * F * R	CGI = % consideration * % market share * 100

Imagine and write down your thoughts on how creating a product or service for that market might affect your current revenues (positively or negatively):

_____

_____

_____

_____

_____

_____

_____

_____

Download a printable PDF of all notes pages at magnani.com/book

DAY 10

Take time to write the full story.

Brace yourself.
Day 10 is a long chapter. But there's no math involved.

Innovation is never a technology problem.

Real innovation doesn't incrementally improve an existing behavior—it presents new opportunities entirely. If we can first envision and map out a more satisfying emotional experience, ultimately technology finds a way.

Stories are the fundamental way we learn and connect emotionally, as people. Deriving inspiration from Joseph Campbell and traditional design thinking alike, our Narrative-Based Innovation process uses detailed storytelling to create a deeper understanding and empathy with customers, to create and communicate a more compelling vision of how to solve their challenges and, ultimately, to deliver more engaging customer experiences.

What is narrative-based innovation?

We've taken an already powerful concept—design thinking—and infused it more deeply with storytelling.

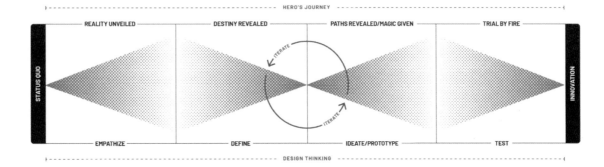

Empathize
Embracing our customers as heroes

This immersive, curiosity-fueled step allows us to understand and document the first chapter in the story. We introduce our heroes with detailed, dimensional personas. Brought to life with stories that reveal who they are, we unveil what rational and emotional motivations affect their behaviors. We weigh the resources and constraints that affect their decisions. And we pore over the joys, frustrations and hardships they experience as they travel on their daily journeys through the world.

Define
Expressing our heroes' needs

We define the challenge we will solve for our heroes not by listing technical or functional requirements, per se, but by declaring as our goal the emotional requirements—the way we want our heroes to feel about themselves and their world after engaging with our solution. In our narrative framework, that means we present that challenge in our heroes' voices. That could be a call for help, an emotional need, a want or need for a desired outcome, or all of the above.

Ideate
Imagining a new world

To generate the greatest number of viable solutions to the challenges our heroes face today and into the future, we leverage the collective intelligence of futurists, trend experts, industry experts, internal and external strategists, and key stakeholders to brainstorm solutions at scale. Through a guided process, we move from the unhindered expression of hundreds of concepts to the prioritization and deep development of the most viable solutions in a very short time. The best solutions are demonstrated and tested through, and documented within, idealized stories of our heroes' encounters and engagements with our solutions, and the resulting outcomes.

Prototype
Forging the solution

We prototype and iterate, early and often. This is trial by fire. We bring the best ideas to life through low-, medium-, and high-fidelity prototypes and test them in the hands of people. It's the only way to truly craft and refine real-world solutions that evoke emotional connections and outcomes equal to those documented in our idealized narratives.

Test

Finally, we bring innovations and prototypes to life, launching the story throughout the organization and the experiences to our real-world heroes, the customers. We do this with every concept, every experience—active and measurable. Whether we're launching an internal vision communications piece, a live-market beta test, or a communications campaign, we know the story is successful when stakeholders and customers become not simply participants but evangelists.

Why storytelling matters.

Sometimes, words are worth a thousand wireframes.

Before we ideate ... Before we prototype ... We write stories. These stories are detailed narratives that walk through the user journey, step by step, annotated with context, motivation and expectation. Why take the time with this step? Because it helps us to more efficiently and effectively create truly unique and delightful user experiences.

Story is the best way to generate, evaluate, and communicate complex experiences.

Stories are the basis for how we learn. Generations have passed down important information to the next generation through stories. We apply these same storytelling principles to create a deeper understanding and empathy with customers to solve their problems and help organizations rally around that vision.

Stories convey vision without a limiting design.

During the initial ideation and brainstorming phase of development, a well-crafted story can convey all required or desired points of interaction without unduly limiting a designer's imagination.

Stories document emotional expectations.

If a technical spec conveys how an experience should be physically coded and deployed, and a functional spec conveys the interactions that code should facilitate, a story can be thought of as the emotional requirements documentation. What points in the user journey should elicit joy or delight? What points require thoughtful decision-making? Which offer relief?

Stories can present future innovations unconstrained by current limitations.

The process of storytelling gives us the freedom to envision a radically disruptive user experience that may seem to be beyond currently available tools or resources. We believe that if you can create a compelling vision, technology eventually finds a way.

Storytelling forces prioritization.

A story is a road map for the visual hierarchy to come in the final experience design. Those interface items or experiences that are critical to forwarding the narrative should, in theory, be featured more prominently in the final user-experience (UX) design. Those elements that are unnecessary to the story should be minimized or considered for removal entirely.

Storytelling exposes the holes.

The simple act of clearly describing a user's journey through an online experience forces the author to resolve abstractions in the requirements.

If you can't explain it to a 6-year-old ...

Simply put, the act of creating and communicating a story that anyone can understand and follow forces clarification of thought. In the design process, a compelling story inspires exploration of new ideas, untethered by perceived organizational or technical constraints.

Ultimately, if the story you craft cannot engage, inspire, and motivate your customers and employees, the end product probably won't either.

So, what are the elements of a compelling innovation story?

All great stories follow a similar arc.

H. Porter Abbott, a professor emeritus in the English department at the University of California, Santa Barbara, calls the preference for linear storytelling "a fundamental operating procedure of the mind." At around 3 years old, our brains begin to compartmentalize sensory information from the world around us into the components of an ongoing narrative, with each of us at the center. He says, "We view our lives as a series of actions, causes, and effects that together form an ongoing story."

In his seminal work, "The Hero with a Thousand Faces," Joseph Campbell lays out the basic structure most (if not all) great stories follow. The Hero's Journey, as Campbell calls it, follows a predictable story arc that (I'll summarize) presents our humble protagonist as an ordinary citizen, reveals a great secret, introduces them to a mentor who calls our hero to fulfill a destiny, then follows that hero on the journey of discovery, challenge and conquest, and, ultimately, home to a world, and the hero, now forever changed. Here, we use Campbell's framework as the jumping-off point for the narrative innovation process.

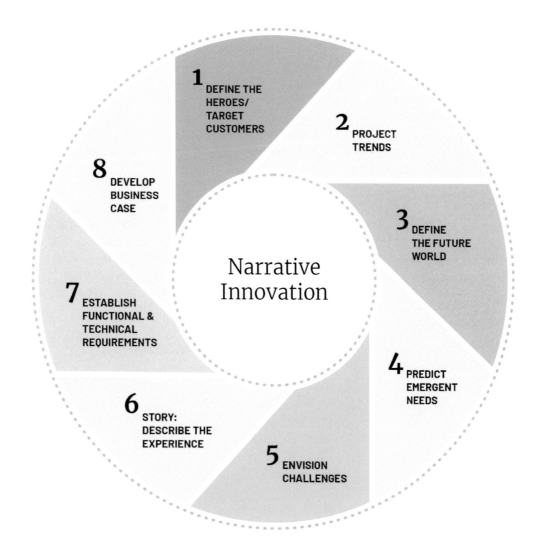

The framework of Joseph Campbell's Hero's Journey helps to create a more compelling narrative foundation for ideating and innovating new products and services.

Innovation stories cast the user as the hero.

In any innovation story, the most important element is your customer or user—aka the hero. Where did they come from, who are they, and why are they the way they are? What human needs and desires are as yet unmet in their world. Or, better yet, in what aspects does their ordinary world cry out for an extraordinary experience? To truly empathize with our hero, we rely on myriad quantitative and qualitative research methodologies: focus groups, ethnographic research, interviews, reading everything and anything about their sources of joy and misery, studying their aspirations across other categories, and how they talk about those challenges. Ultimately, you want to create a fully dimensional character sketch with as much physical detail and emotional motivation as possible. The more your innovators feel they know and understand the hero, the more likely the solution you create will have personal and emotional value to the user in the end.

Imagine your business or brand as the mentor.

In Campbell's framework, the hero always encounters and befriends a mentor, e.g., Gandalf, Obi-Wan, Dumbledore, Willy Wonka, etc. This mentor has the responsibility of not only revealing the true nature of the world to the hero but also helping the hero to understand how, with the mentor's guidance, they can accomplish something extraordinary. A great innovation story positions the brand as a force in service to the user. It's not unlike Clayton Christensen's "Jobs to be done" perspective on branding.

Define the quest.

It's easy, and all too common, for companies to define their customers' challenges in terms of the products they sell to them. But a great innovation story defines the challenge in human terms. Improving the hero's self-esteem. Heightening satisfaction. Reducing anxiety. Empowering growth. Improving social or emotional interpersonal connections. An emotional foundation to the definition of the challenge allows for greater creativity and freedom of exploration in the ideation stage. In the end, it should also lead to innovations with greater emotional resonance for the hero.

Build the world revealed to them.

To craft a world detailed enough to inform the innovation process, you'll need to understand what new products and services are on the horizon, and how analogous products have changed your target segment in the past. We often leverage the collective intelligence of futurists, trend experts, industry experts, internal and external strategists, and key internal stakeholders from within our clients' organizations to begin to build a working model of the world "at launch." How far out that world is, chronologically speaking, depends on the time horizon of the strategic vision as well as the traditional development cycle of the business. In crafting the model of that world, project how key factors (economic, cultural, generational, social, technological, etc.) that influence our hero's journey in relation to the problem you are trying to solve may change. Document what new opportunities will result from the progression of those trends. Then, incorporate the most relevant aspects of those features into your innovation story.

Explain the magic your next product or service will create.

In every hero's journey, the mentor reveals some hidden and powerful magic to the hero. In your story, detail the ways in which the hero's life will be enhanced by meaningful encounters with your business or brand. The point here is to define the emotional requirements of the solution in terms of benefits, not features, and their relevance to the hero's journey. You don't need to spell out the specific tools, products or services—that comes later. Obi-Wan helped Luke trust the force. Willy Wonka helped Charlie rise above the seven deadly sins. Dumbledore helped Harry understand the value in self-sacrifice. It's these big-picture issues, once understood, that make evaluations of the value various ideas generated much less subjective.

Write your innovation story.

Once you have all of the elements defined, it's time to develop the actual narrative—the story of the hero, facing challenges in the world you created. We've seen that the more realized and dimensional you can make that world, the more numerous, compelling and innovative the resulting ideas will be. And that makes all the difference in the world.

Three Compelling Uses for Narrative-Based Innovation

The more unfamiliar the destination, the more a strong narrative adds value.

Earlier in this chapter, we talked about the value of narrative storytelling in the innovation process. In this chapter, we'll cover what types of projects benefit most from this approach and why. Evaluating when and why this approach makes sense is actually fairly simple. The greater the unknowns, the greater the value of a story. A design-thinking exercise around refining an existing product category will benefit from storytelling, to be sure, but not as much as design thinking around creating an entirely new category altogether.

The narrative is the first prototype.

A great innovation narrative immerses the reader into its world and allows for a detailed exposition of the desired interactions, features and benefits, using no more technology than the written word. In the final section of this chapter, we cover the three most compelling uses of Narrative-Based Innovation and explain how we use storytelling to accelerate and mitigate risks.

01. Innovating new products and services

Innovating new products and services is the classic innovation application. And storytelling, in some sense, has always been a part of this process, usually establishing context or framing need. But in Narrative-Based Innovation, storytelling takes on a more substantive role. In Narrative-Based Innovation, the story is far more detailed, documenting a journey through the user experience, and documenting the functional and emotional requirements of an innovation long before any design or technology resources need to be applied.

For example, the greater the depth and clarity a detailed narrative brings to a concept, the better an engineer can envision the full experience and purpose of a new product or service as they focus and prioritize efforts. Management can more quickly and clearly articulate across departments or to the board, not only what the new product or service is but also how it will be experienced by customers. And sales teams can familiarize themselves with real-world use cases before they actually occur.

02. Expanding into new markets.

So, you're considering promoting innovative new uses for your product or service. After you've performed all necessary quantitative evaluations of a potential market expansion (e.g., market size, price elasticity, cost of customer acquisition, just to name a few), incorporating those details into detailed customer journey narratives, complete with exploration of intent, desire, and need can give you a better sense whether those numbers are a conservative estimate or wishful thinking. Can you draft an obviously believable story? Or, does the exposition of the user journey require dubious leaps of logic?

03. Exploring viability of entirely new behaviors.

Unlike the previous use case that involves innovating new uses for existing resources, this is about exploring the viability or feasibility of altogether new behaviors. Let's take, for example, the recent explorations in the ride-sharing space where ordinary folks, through a mobile app, offer their personal vehicle up for rental to, or rental from, total strangers.

Using Narrative-Based Innovation as the innovation framework, long before prototyping an app interface or building out a business pro forma, you would craft a series of detailed narratives that explore the motivations, risks, opportunities and threats involved. The act of detailing the behaviors can continue to refine and accelerate the modeling and iterating of the user experience, as well as help accelerate the building of a consensus vision for the future among stakeholders.

It's always about perspective.

If we have learned anything from science fiction and fantasy writers through the ages, it's that when we create a sufficiently compelling vision, technology finds a way. And Narrative-Based Innovation is about taking time to explore, iterate, test, and refine that vision as much as possible, at the most human-centered experiential level, so when the final narrative presents a truly compelling vision, the path from concept to offering appears straight and obvious.

Start building an innovation story one element at a time.

The Hero: Describe your best customer today. Describe the problem you solve for your best customers.

_____

_____

_____

_____

_____

The Antagonist: Describe the disruptive competitor that will attack your business in the next three years. What technology will enable that disruption?

_____

_____

_____

_____

_____

The Challenge: Describe how your current offering fails your best/most loyal customers.

_____

_____

_____

_____

_____

The Environment: Describe the key external risk factors and trends (technological, generational, cultural, competitive) your business will face over the next 3–5 years.

The Goal: Describe the world in which your customers' challenges are overcome.

The Revelation: How to get started: If you could invest 10% of revenue for the next 3–5 years on innovation, describe how you would spend it.

Describe what would help to embed innovation into your company culture (think about what internal roles or functions would have to exist or change).

Download a printable PDF of all notes pages at magnani.com/book

DAY 11

Use story to examine failures, too.

Some stories just can't end well.

Let's start with the story of MoviePass. If you're unfamiliar, MoviePass is the app-based subscription service that, at least originally, let moviegoers see one movie a day at the theater for one low monthly fee. As of this writing, to say the service has been experiencing growing pains, of late, would be a generous characterization. If you didn't listen to Episode 9 of the Magnani podcast "Brilliant", spoiler alert, I don't believe they're going to pull out of their very public tailspin. And it's not because of their numerous, recent, also very public, customer service missteps.

The narrative lessons of MoviePass.

When you start evaluating MoviePass through the lens of Narrative-Based Innovation, it becomes clear that, had MoviePass taken the time to develop a detailed narrative—walking through the consumer buying process and exploring the purchase setting, as well as the emotions and motivations of the customer in the process— the story just doesn't hold water.

The customer as protagonist.

In our full process, we would create detailed narratives, naming our protagonist(s), examining their environments, their broader day-to-day experiences, their nuanced decision-making processes, etc. But for the purposes of this discussion, I'll simply outline the basic and obvious inputs and outputs that would go into the story. In the case of MoviePass, it really should suffice.

Whether we choose a casual moviegoer or a diehard theater patron as our protagonist, once we examine consumer habits, it becomes difficult to draft a narrative in which MoviePass makes much sense for most consumers.

MoviePass has undergone a number of pricing/service incarnations since its founding in 2011, each apparently losing money. However, the most notoriety came in August of 2017, when MoviePass introduced a plan priced at $9.99 a month that would allow users to see up to one movie a day—which, if you don't stop to examine the real-world use cases, seems like quite a deal. But as we begin to write out the narrative of average users, the economics seem less appealing.

Americans attend, on average, a little over five movies a year at the theater. Unless you assume our protagonist's consumption rate would double, it's difficult to craft a successful customer journey narrative that doesn't require massive leaps in logic. Even at double the average rate, MoviePass is still ultimately a money-losing proposition for most consumers. Not surprisingly, it also proved a money-losing proposition for MoviePass. Why? Allow me to speculate a bit.

In general, I believe markets are, on average, rational. Meaning that casual moviegoers did the math on the $9.99 plan and realized it would cost more than simply buying tickets whenever they wanted to see a movie. So, who signed up? Heavy users who are also good at math and, in fact, getting more than they pay for in comparison to simply purchasing movie tickets ad hoc, movie by movie, theater by theater. The downside for MoviePass was that they were paying the theater full price for every ticket, which was as high as $15 in major metro areas, regardless of what the user paid.

So, the only purchase stories that made sense to consumers seemed not to offer any possibility of a happy ending for MoviePass. The truth of which we see laid out below.

JUST HOW OFTEN TO MOST AMERICANS GO OUT TO THE MOVIES?

American Adults' Movie-Going Trends • January 2014 • % of respondents aged 18+

	ALL ADULTS	18-36	37-48	49-67	68+	MALE	FEMALE
WENT TO ANY MOVIE	68%	83%	73%	59%	44%	70%	66%
WENT TO 10+ MOVIES	17%	24%	21%	11%	9%	20%	14%
MEAN NUMBER ATTENDED	4.8	6.3	5.3	3.6	3.2	5.5	4.1
PREFER WATCHING MOVIES AT HOME	57%	52%	56%	60%	60%	53%	60%
AGREE: I AM GOING TO THE MOVIES LESS OFTEN NOW THAN A FEW YEARS AGO	66%	67%	59%	66%	74%	61%	70%

Source: https://www.marketingcharts.com/[10]

[10] https://www.marketingcharts.com/wp-content/uploads/2014/01/Harris-Americans-Movie-Going-Trends-Jan2014.png

MoviePass—a script that should have never made it out of development.

Over the course of the company's history, it's fair to say, MoviePass could never get its story straight. It struggled to sign up 20,000 members at its original $30-per-month movie-a-day offering. But the membership quickly ballooned to over a million after MoviePass lowered the fee to just $9.99 per month in August of 2017.

The story MoviePass was spinning among the press was that, while they were losing money on every ticket, they would eventually make it up from the sale of user data.

But, again, that story requires a massive leap in logic. By comparison, at the end of 2017, Facebook was generating roughly $6 per quarter on every user. That would imply that if MoviePass were ever to become cash-flow positive, its members would need to be eight times as valuable to advertisers as Facebook users.

Projected Facebook revenue per user per year[11] = ~$6.18 (per quarter) * 4 = $24.56

Hypothetical MoviePass cost per user = $8.90 (average US ticket price, 2017) * 3 (movies per month) * 12 (months) = $320

MoviePass revenue per user @ $9.99 (per month) * 12 = $119.88

Net income per user = -$200.12

Which should explain why MoviePass, in this model, was burning through nearly $73 million a month.

Pay no attention to the man behind the curtain.

In an August 15, 2018, letter to MoviePass members, Mitch Lowe, CEO, tried to quiet members' fears or anger at the company, saying, "The truth is, disruption and innovation require staying flexible and having an open mind."[12]

The response that popped into my mind was, yes, keep an open mind but not so open that your brains fall out. The company portrays itself as the hero in an epic, when it is, from the outside, looking more like a tragedy.

A blast from the past: the story of Microsoft "BOB."

As another example of how going through the process of developing and evaluating the plausibility of a customer-journey narrative might have prevented abject market failure, let's take a look at the story of Microsoft BOB.

[11] https://www.cnbc.com/2018/01/31/facebook-earnings-q4-2017-arpu.html
[12] https://mailchi.mp/moviepass/please-read-updates-to-your-moviepass-plan

In 1995, Microsoft was looking to expand the audience for personal computers by creating a more friendly, limited-option interface called "BOB." On the surface, BOB made sense. There was a large segment of the population who were casually interested in computers but were intimidated, confused, or uninspired by the existing Windows desktop interface. But, had Microsoft taken the time to develop a detailed narrative, walking through the consumer buying process and exploring the purchase setting as well as the emotions and motivations in the process, I have to believe they would not have launched.

For context, in 1995, presenting the animated BOB interface actually required more computing and graphics horsepower than presenting the standard Windows interface. Further, BOB was sold shrink-wrapped in a box at a cost of $99. In effect, the company was betting that a casual user, heretofore unable to mentally justify the purchase price of a low-end standard computer, would actually pay a premium for a more powerful machine, plus the additional price of the BOB software, for an end result that offered a more limited computing experience. The leaps of logic necessary to make that journey believable are, at best, heroic.

The main view of Microsoft: BvOB

It's always smart to craft, examine, and test user-journey narratives.

Put them in front of unbiased consumers, industry experts, channel partners, guys on the sales floor, etc. Listen to their feedback. If your narrative doesn't pass the believability smell test, work the business, product, and pricing details until it does.

Examine a past business failure or disappointment from the customer or user perspective.

Imagine their motivations, expectations and experiences as they approached your offering. Imagine the gaps in expectation from both party's perspectives.

Download a printable PDF of all notes pages at magnani.com/book

DAY
12

Beware "good enough."

Should you really be worried about "good enough?"

Consumers increasingly expect good, fast, and cheap. As new technologies lower barriers to entry to many industries, the price/value equation skews dramatically toward the lowest margin position, and consumers often feel like they can find a satisfactory mix of good, fast, and cheap. Or, at least, "good enough." When this happens, all too often the incumbent players in the market either don't see the threat looming or they dismiss it as insignificant, until it's too late. Let's see what lessons we can learn when examining the rise of YouTube™ over the past decade and a few competitive responses from within the television industry.

"Good enough" never looks threatening—at first.

Imagine you were a television producer in 2006 and someone showed you one of the first viral videos, "Myahee."

You couldn't be blamed for watching this lip-sync performance and dismissing this new user-generated video phenomenon as posing no threat to your business model. But as the technology quickly and continually improved, and high-definition cameras were built into nearly every mobile computing device, production quality, which was formerly reserved for local broadcast television stations, was suddenly dropped firmly into the hands of virtually anyone who had the desire and time to create video content. Game on.

"Good enough" emerges at unappealing scale.

When this field of new creators was unleashed on us all, they didn't even come close to commanding the kind of viewing audiences of even the worst-performing show on the worst-performing cable TV channel. But most of them, fueled by creative passion, would have posted videos for no audience at all. And, as passion is at times contagious, some of those audiences became large enough to generate ad views and commensurate real life-enhancing, if not sustaining, income. The opportunity attracted more and more creators who were serving more and more niche markets with more and more content. This eventually resulted in a critical mass of tagged, related, and suggested content that was capable of keeping a viewer discovering and engaged for hours at a time. And, more critically for our aforementioned television executive, these creators began to influence the default viewing behaviors of the new generation who were growing up online.

"Good enough" chips away at traditional markets.

As Gen Z grew up watching online video—most of it firmly entrenched in the "good enough" level of production—the connection to traditional television waned. In fact, more than 50% of Gen Z can't live without YouTube.[13] And, according to a poll published in 2016, 30% plan on cutting out cable television services altogether.[14]

[13] https://www.adweek.com/digital/infographic-50-of-gen-z-cant-live-without-youtube-and-other-stats-that-will-make-you-feel-old/
[14] https://www.businessinsider.com/cord-cutting-intentions-2016-3

Three smart responses to "good enough."

The democratization of technology obviously isn't limited to video creation or consumption. This type of threat can affect any industry. But the following three strategic responses by incumbents within the video industry can serve well as templates for just about any industry.

01. "Mind the gap."

Facing the flood of ubiquitous, shareable, "good enough" video content, industry behemoths HBO® and Netflix have doubled down on quality and exclusivity. Further, HBO broadened its distribution, first, via the HBO GO® app tied to its traditional cable subscriptions and eventually to HBO NOW®, an app-based subscription that requires no accompanying cable TV subscription.

Netflix followed a parallel path to HBO, pivoting from a content distributor to a content creator with exclusive series like the Emmy Award-winning "House of Cards," "Orange Is the New Black," and a number of Marvel Universe-based superhero shows, just to name a few.

The main takeaway here is that when barriers to entry become low enough, any market will inevitably become flooded with competitors at the low end. A clever tagline or ad campaign in most cases won't help you protect your margins. A more viable position is to, in effect, re-raise the barrier to entry. In the case of HBO and Netflix, that was the level of production value/expense, but the idea applies to any business.

There is no shortage of online retailers competing on price and selection. So, Amazon raised the barrier by investing in logistics and distribution. There is no shortage of providers of homeowners' insurance, so Lemonade[15] invested in machine learning and AI to deliver an unprecedented easy purchasing experience. When the market gets "cheap," invest in creating a differentiating, difficult-to-copy advantage.

02. "Do as the Romans do."

When early YouTube users started uploading snippets of their favorite TV shows, movies, and music, the initial (predictable) response from copyright holders was to try and shut it down through DCMA notices, etc. Over time, some of the more progressive copyright holders realized many of these posts could be used to promote more traditional outlets for their intellectual property, and working with YouTube, they could help monetize those uploads through advertising revenue.

In this strategy, the smart move was to look for ways to use the momentum of a seemingly overwhelming force to profitable advantage. If the threat looks like an infinite game of whack-a-mole, you're better off dropping the sledgehammer and putting some corporate swag on the mole and using it to hawk your wares.

[15] https://www.lemonade.com

In the end, numbers are numbers, and large audiences command real advertiser dollars, which in turn attract the most deep-pocketed of incumbents. In 2013, DreamWorks Animation paid $33 million for YouTube channel AwesomenessTV. Warner Bros.® placed an $18 million bet on YouTube video game channel Machinima. Even Disney eventually placed $950 million down on Maker Studios, best known at the time as the company behind "Epic Rap Battles of History" and (the now highly controversial) PewDiePie.

While this strategy can be, and has been, successful, waiting for an emerging market to mature and then purchasing an emerging competitor, already standing at the end of a well-worn path to success, can reduce market uncertainty—but you should be aware that confidence inevitably comes at a premium price.

Incumbent, disrupt thyself.

Ultimately, the smartest strategy in the face of emerging technologies is always to ask one question: "How could a new market entrant use this to disrupt my business?" Then, do that. If you don't, eventually someone else will.

What are the top five threats to my market share?

Are there emerging technologies beginning to take less-desirable market share?

How could a new market entrant use an emerging technology to attract my best customers and disrupt my business?

Download a printable PDF of all notes pages at magnani.com/book

DAY 13

Rip success from the jaws of failure.

Innovate. Activate. Accelerate.

Let's go back: February 6, 2018.

The successful launch of the Falcon Heavy by SpaceX and the landing of two of its three booster rockets marked a milestone for the company and for spaceflight. The visuals were amazing ("Starman" in a Tesla ... twin booster rocket touchdowns ... are you kidding me?). But more interesting than the launch itself were the comments from SpaceX co-founder Elon Musk the day before the launch. When asked what he thought the odds of success would be, this is what he told the reporter from ArsTechnica:[16]

"There's a lot that could go wrong," Musk admitted. "A really tremendous amount. I really like to emphasize that the odds of success are not super high. I don't want to jinx it—I'm tempted to say. Because I feel super optimistic. But I feel as though that optimism has no basis in fact. I feel like we've got a two-thirds chance of success, but in reality, we only have a 50-50 chance."

A 50-50 chance? Musk was comfortable watching at least $90 million go up in a ball of flames. In fact, he was expecting it. That sentiment gets to the heart of prototyping and its critical role in innovation.

Even the best ideas are worthless speculation until you make something.

SpaceX was founded in 2002 with the goal of becoming a commercially viable company in an industry known for massive cost overruns. To be viable, they had to lower the cost of each launch. Early on, the SpaceX team seized on a key aspect of spaceflight that bloated the costs: the rocket hardware itself. Booster rockets—the key piece of machinery that catapults a payload into orbit—had historically been ditched in the ocean. The salvageable boosters that didn't sink to the bottom of the sea, completely lost, were soaked in seawater—meaning the entire system, including the massively complex engines, needed to be disassembled, cleaned, inspected, and reassembled before the rocket could be used again. SpaceX had a novel idea: Why don't we land the boosters back on Earth after they've completed their job?

A great idea, but SpaceX would need to prove it would work before anyone would contract them to fling their hardware into orbit around Earth. How would they prove it? Prototypes.

Many, many prototypes. Computer models. Component tests. Small test launches. Full-scale test flights. Some of these tests were successful. But most of them were failures, because they were designed to be. In fact, SpaceX proudly released a video compiling some of their more spectacular failures.

[16] https://arstechnica.com/science/2018/02/at-the-pad-elon-musk-sizes-up-the-falcon-heavys-chance-of-success/

New software, new hardware, or new concepts very rarely hit their mark perfectly on the first try. But failure can be revelatory and often provides more opportunities to perfect a product than success. In examining the root cause of a design failure, the product steadily improves.

Take your idea on a test flight

At Magnani, we're not launching rockets. So, what can we take away from this example? To us, it comes down to three basic rules:

01. Test early. Test often.

As early as you can in the process, run strategic, UX, and creative concepts past colleagues who have no view on the project. Does this make sense? Is it telling the story you want to tell? What does your colleague think project team members should do next?

As the project continues to evolve, check back in with those same individuals and slot in more research with real users. Have the refinements we've made addressed your challenges? Is this a smoother experience? Are we better at communicating the narrative?

02. Embrace the explosions.

When you get feedback that completely contradicts your assumptions, don't be defensive or dismissive. Embrace the feedback. Examine what you missed. Were there biases in your team that may have blinded you to a better solution? Has a process or narrative become overcomplicated and obscured the true objective of the project or deliverables?

Once you've uncovered the reason for your errors, document them in a way that other teams can learn from and build upon your experiences. In this way, those teams can avoid experiencing the same pitfalls in the future and, instead, move your practice forward.

03. Fail forward.

SpaceX has steadily failed forward for the past 16 years. They've failed their way to successfully launching the world's most powerful rocket and sticking the landing of two of three rocket boosters.

Oh, wait ... did I mention the third booster slammed into the Atlantic Ocean at upward of 300 mph, annihilating the rocket and damaging the drone ship it was supposed to land on?

Looks like SpaceX still has some more to learn.

Recall the greatest failure in your company history. What did you learn from it?

What were the reactions within the company to that failure?

Were there outcomes that could have been different if the failure had been viewed as a learning opportunity?

There is no silver bullet. It's silver buckshot. Everything is marketing.

–Rudy Magnani

What will you connect?

Our fractured media environment, together with accelerating technological advances, is making it more difficult than ever to gain traction in the marketplace. This section of the book provides examples of strategies, tactics, technologies and target market considerations to help you rethink, reimagine and revitalize your activation strategies.

DAY
14

Learn marketing from Jack Nicholson.

Great marketing advice from "Mulholland Man" Jack.

To maintain a career in Hollywood over a period of more than five decades takes a singular dedication to maintaining and promoting your brand. Although he might be the last person to admit to being something as pedestrian as a marketer, Jack Nicholson has, over the years, presented to the world a number of bon mots that would serve any marketer well as guideposts for improving their marketing acumen.

"With my sunglasses on, I'm Jack Nicholson. Without them, I'm fat and 60."

What Jack is highlighting here is that a brand presented with consistency creates value over and above the spec sheet. Jack understands that his logo, while it may go through redesign every few years, follows a consistent style guide.

"Because you know, down deep in my heart, when all is said and done, I still live under the illusion that basically people think of me as an up-and-coming young actor."

Know your positioning, live it, and stick with it. Jack's positioning as an "up-and-coming young actor" gave him greater opportunity to pick and choose roles, as everyone knows up-and-coming actors are always exploring. For brands, the stronger and narrower the positioning, the greater the chances the consumers you wish to transact with will seek you out, just like directors would seek out Mr. Nicholson for those more exploratory roles.

"There is no way you can get people to believe you on screen if they know who you really are through television."

There are two great takeaways from this quote. First: Your distribution channel is your positioning. Just as it's tough to be a film star when people think of you as a television personality, marketers have to weigh every distribution expansion opportunity against the potential impact that channel can have on the perception of the brand. You're not a luxury brand if you're sold at big-box retail. Or, at least, you won't be for long. Second: Every violation of the brand promise eats away at value. Again, Jack understands that his brand is composed of the performances he creates on the big screen. Every television interview or paparazzi moment exposing the "real" Jack Nicholson detracts from the curated big-screen brand persona. For marketers, it means there are no harmless violations of brand—no matter how small. Every time the style guides are broken on a PowerPoint presentation; each time a logo is stretched out of proportion on a trade show tchotchke; each time someone in accounting makes their own program book ad in Microsoft Word. Every little thing can chip away at the image and understanding of the brand.

"I wanted to be the best actor possible. I worked very hard at the craft of it."

Much like Jack's acting talents, great brands are not built overnight. Building one requires hard, coordinated work, involving the spectrum of disciplines. You need to codify and quantify the impression of the brand among internal stakeholders, potential targets, and its stature relative to the competitive set. You need to use research to understand and establish the core values you believe communicate the brand in terms that are consistent with organizational capabilities and that resonate within the marketplace. You need to translate those values into a brand positioning that conveys the greatest value, differentiation, and competitive advantage of the organization. And then you bring that brand idea to life—designing logos, developing brand standards and guidelines, creating internal and external communications and messaging platforms, refining interdepartmental processes, developing marketing communications, spearheading product ideation and innovation, analyzing market sizing and segmentation, and implementing strategic plans. Whew. Maybe we all should have tried acting.

"Almost everybody's happy to be a fool for love."

Perhaps spoken with an air of dramatic irony by our friend Jack. But in marketing, so true. Great brands, executed flawlessly over time, engender among their customers a near irrational affinity. The customers have no idea the blood, sweat and tears marketers put into making it seem natural, even effortless.

But those brands that deliver on their promise and remain customer-focused, consistently, over time, can make unreasonable demands of those customers, and those customers thank them for it. It's no small coincidence that when adding the word "sheeple" (meaning people who are docile, compliant, or easily influenced) to the dictionary, the folks at Merriam-Webster provided the following reference to customers of the alpha brand, Apple as an example of its use:

"Apple's debuted a battery case for the juice-sucking iPhone—an ungainly lumpy case the sheeple will happily shell out $99 for." –Doug Criss"

"The minute that you're not learning, I believe you're dead."

Probably the best advice for marketers that Mr. Nicholson has ever given. We all need to keep learning. About our customers. About our competitors. About the marketplace. About new technologies. About emerging trends. If we can keep that top of mind, the rest will come much easier.

Write a letter to Jack Nicholson, thanking him for all of his great marketing advice.

This won't help your business. But you can always tell your friends you're pen pals with Jack Nicholson. http://www.jack-nicholson.info/contact/

Say every one of the above quotes using your best Jack Nicholson impression. Come on. *You know you have one.*

Again, this won't help your business. But your Jack Nicholson impression can always use more practice. The bonus: You will also find yourself with a passing Christian Slater impression by proxy.

Download a printable PDF of all notes pages at magnani.com/book

DAY
15

Wield influence responsibly.

Just to be clear, influencer marketing is not new.

In the mid-1960s, when Lee Iacocca was General Manager of Ford, he was preparing to launch the new Mustang onto the American public. Legend has it that as part of the marketing program, Iacocca placed Mustangs in the hands of "big man on campus" types at colleges and universities across the country to jump-start the new model's cool factor. Today, influencer marketing is common practice for a growing portion of marketing budgets, with brands expected to spend as much as $5-10 billion with influencers by 2020. You could say that with social media influencers, marketing has been taken to scale.

If you haven't yet taken the influencer-marketing plunge, it's time to cover some of the basics:

What are the FTC regulations governing influencer marketing?

Why is this the first question? If you have never done influencer-marketing campaigns, this is an easy (and potentially costly) point to overlook. The FTC requires all influencers to disclose any sponsorships near the top of any post. The FTC has an online endorsement[17] guide in an easy-to-follow Q&A format. Protecting yourself and your influencers is easy, but you need to understand the constraints.

How do you find influencers in the first place?

According to the Linqia State of Influencer Marketing Report 2017[18], 64% of respondents engage dedicated management companies (Linqia being one example) to provide turnkey influencer programs.

[17] https://www.ftc.gov/tips-advice/business-center/guidance/ftcs-endorsement-guides-what-people-are-asking
[18] http://www.linqia.com/wp-content/uploads/2016/11/The-State-of-Influencer-Marketing-2017_Final-Report.pdf

How do you distinguish between reach and influence?

In its simplest form, reach is equal to the number of followers or subscribers that are exposed to an influencer's content. Some may add secondary reach numbers, e.g., populations exposed to re-shares. But anyone can buy followers, or the appearance of reach. So, neither of those numbers really quantifies influence. To quantify influence, you need to do a little homework beyond the raw numbers:

- What percentage of the influencer's audience meets your target customer profile?

- What percentage of the content they produce is relevant to your industry and target customers?

- Does the influencer achieve more or less engagement when they're delivering content relevant to your industry or business?

- Do they command a similar presence across platforms?

How do influencers get paid?

There are a number of methods, each with its pros and cons. Some favor success on the influencer end of the funnel; others favor success on the marketer's end of the funnel.

- **Free products or services**—you want the influencer to talk about something, you give them that particular something for free. This is generally better suited to one-off campaigns, product launches, etc.

- **Pay per post (PPP)**—a set fee paid to the influencer for each blog article or social post linking to your site. Easy to verify, but it assumes all posts have equal value, regardless of their effectiveness.

- **Cost per engagement (CPE)**—a set fee for every click, share, forward, et al. This model begins to distinguish between the relative values of various posts but is more cumbersome to track and doesn't tie back well to downstream business metrics.

- **Cost per click (CPC)**—a set fee is paid to the influencer for every click through to your site. It addresses the issue of relative value based on effectiveness of the posts to generate clicks but stops short of rewarding for the quality of the customer delivered.

- **Cost per acquisition (CPA)**—a fee is paid only when someone an influencer has directed toward the site converts to a customer, e.g., subscriptions or sales. This definitely favors the marketer as it limits the ultimate cost per acquisition.

How do you measure ROI (Return on Influence)?

So, after you choose a cost model, how do you tie it back to success measures? The short answer: The closer your metrics get to an actual monetary transaction, the greater your ability to calculate true ROI. Now, for the longer answer: If your goal is increased awareness, you can run pre- and post-campaign awareness surveys. But it's probably impossible to tease out the incremental effect of an individual influencer outside of the broader marketing you're performing.

If you're looking for something more concrete, like page views, supplying influencer-specific tracking URLs tied into your analytics package, or creating influencer-specific landing pages will do the trick. That will at least get you to understand what those specific clicks and views are costing you.

Delving even more deeply into the analytics, you can track specific events to see how deeply the influencer-delivered users are engaged. Ultimately, if you assign a specific dollar value to specific engagement points, confirmed active leads, or final transactions, and you can review your analytics to track those leads back to specific influencers, you can quickly come very close to quantifying exact percentage returns on dollars spent.

Bonus question: Should you trust your brand to a third party?

The simple answer is that your brand is already being talked about online. So, assuming you're transparent about the sponsored nature of your influencer relationships, proactively guiding the conversation into positive territory can only be beneficial. Just take the time to understand who those influencers are and what the depth of their influence is. Also, make sure your compensation method aligns with your business goals and analytics capabilities. The rest should feel like a great conversation.

What percentage of your customers use social media to find information about products or services in your industry?

Who are the key influencers in your industry space?

What (if anything) are those influencers saying about your brand/products/services?

What measure(s) could you use to objectively gauge the success of any influencer strategy?

Download a printable PDF of all notes pages at magnani.com/book

DAY 16

Don't follow the leader.

Most companies make the same five marketing mistakes.

While there are now so many more opportunities to reach customers than there were only 10 years ago, the expansion of options has made decisions on how to improve returns on a limited marketing budget much more complicated. To simplify things, I compiled a shortlist of what, in my experience, are the five most common mistakes businesses make in navigating this complexity. Is your company guilty of any of the following mistakes?

01. Positioning the brand relative to the market leader

For many businesses, it is tempting to think that screaming "Us too!" louder than your competition will be enough to steal share from the market leader. It may, to a small extent, if there's a visible price difference—but usually it won't without their making a dramatic sacrifice in margin or risking swift retaliation. Challenger brands that gain the greatest long-term success define a narrow position around an idea that offers customers an affiliation, experience, or advantage found nowhere else in the market. By doing so, challenger brands avoid price comparisons and command a premium for their offerings.

02. Trying to swallow the elephant whole

Businesses, eager for results, often mistakenly think that increasing their market share requires broadening their target audience. The truth, however, is that pursuing a broader target audience only increases competition. This mistake is the conjoined twin of the positioning mistake outlined above. Trying to serve all of the people all of the time inevitably leads to compromised positioning, an overly complex offering, a confused consumer base, or all of the above.

03. Fighting on too many fronts

Too often, businesses succumb to the temptation of spreading media dollars across a large number of outlets in an attempt to reach all customers, everywhere, all of the time. However, it is generally smarter to maximize your share of voice and create a unique customer experience within a limited number of outlets. Prioritize your media choices against a more limited, high-opportunity customer segment to establish a dominant presence within those highest-priority media outlets. You can convert more sinners by building a compelling church than by speaking quietly on busy street corners.

04. Expecting reward without risk

For businesses' shares to grow, their returns must exceed the market's as a whole. As with any investment, realizing better-than-average returns from marketing spend usually requires taking higher-than-average risks. We aren't advocating reckless abandon, or faith in hunches, but a continuous appetite for setting aside a portion of the budget for taking calculated risks and testing hypotheses as evaluated by metrics. Unexpected opportunities won't uncover themselves.

05. Aiming for #1 share.

Let's look for a moment at every business case writer's favorite company, Apple. The iPhone has a sub-20% share of the smartphone market, yet Apple extracts more than 90% of the industry's profits. As we all should have learned from Richard Miniter's classic, "The Myth of Market Share," competing for share, in and of itself, is a race to low margins. Yet product managers are often bonused on share-of-market increases.

Given Apple's current success in cellphones, it seems counterintuitive to look at them as anything but a leader. But they were the quintessential challenger when they entered the mobile market. You can go through each of the strategy hazards listed above and it's easy to see how Apple consciously avoided all of them.

We've mentioned Apple a number of times in this book. Not because they're innovative—they usually let other companies innovate and test concepts, then adopt the most promising. But when they do adopt a concept, they execute exceptionally well. Avoiding quick wins at the expense of long-term strategy. Following their inner compass. And they managed to take a spot among the largest, most profitable companies in the world.

Which, if any, of the above behaviors does your company exhibit?

If you stopped those behaviors, how would it change your approach to market?

What would you predict the outcome of those changes to be?

Download a printable PDF of all notes pages at magnani.com/book

DAY 17

Ask WTF is ABM?

Planes, Trains, Automobiles and Account-Based Marketing.

It seems like every other large marketing conference has a speaker or a full track about Account-Based Marketing (ABM). If you are a consumer packaged goods (CPG) company selling to broad consumer target markets, you probably shouldn't care. But if you're a business-to-business (B2B) marketer with a line of products or services that potentially sells to various departments within your customers' businesses, you probably should care. Or, at least, care enough to know what it is. So, let's dive in.

It used to be the widget guy sold the widgets ... to everyone he could.

When you walk into traditional marketing and sales departments of a large B2B business, you'll find people and resources divided up against certain practical segments, e.g., industries, products, and channels. That's how we end up with job titles like the one famously presented in the film "Planes, Trains and Automobiles" when John Candy introduces himself as "Del Griffith, American Light and Fixture, Director of Sales, Shower Curtain Ring Division".[19]

Now, we are not faulting Del. He's likely the best shower-curtain-ring man in the business. However, when you consider that American Light and Fixture (AL&F) surely sells more than shower curtain rings, and surely they sell those other things to other people in the same companies that Del visits to sell shower curtain rings, we quickly see inefficiencies in the AL&F sales and marketing approach for larger accounts that need a multitude of solutions from our fixture-selling friends.

ABM is about maximizing key relationships.

With a shift to an ABM approach, B2B marketers identify high-value accounts—those customers in enterprises that have multiple products and services needs across multiple divisions and/or departments—and create dedicated teams and personalized campaigns to support and maximize revenue from them. But as simple as it sounds, it represents a fairly dramatic organizational shift for most B2B sales and marketing organizations.

[19] https://www.youtube.com/watch?v=Rd5dY0HoZS0

ABM is about breaking down barriers between sales and marketing.

In many B2B organizations we've worked with, the sales and marketing departments have been, at best, agreeable neighboring tribes. But frequently their incentives lack alignment and their measures of success are disconnected or mutually exclusive. For an ABM approach to work, sales and marketing need to be following the same plan, tracking the same KPIs and, ultimately, coming to consensus on how best to approach any strategic shifts or opportunities.

From an org-chart view, that means having a single account director at the top of the account team who is responsible for the efforts and performance of the sales and marketing specialists dedicated to the account. They are responsible for the growth and profitability of their accounts and the success of the teams they manage. This combination has a number of distinct advantages for the enterprise:

Increased clarity of success measures and ROI.

Done properly, ABM should allocate specific budget dollars in support of sales and marketing for each key account. Theoretically, creating a dedicated P&L for that account should be fairly cut and dried. Support staff, overhead, and campaigns paid for out of that budget cost the company X dollars, delivered Y dollars of incremental revenue, and Z proposals or pending contracts to the pipeline. The efforts are either working to grow the specific account or they're not, and it should be clear by how much for every dollar spent.

Optimization of efforts and resources.

From the account side, where once a company would have countless Del Griffiths with single-product expertise reaching out to the account—sometimes overlapping the efforts of competing Dels—now they would optimally have a single point of contact managing multiple relationships within the account.

Transformation from vendor to partner.

ABM, by its nature, elevates the marketer's knowledge of its clients' businesses and, more importantly, improves understanding of how the business really operates, day to day. The account support team may actually gain greater visibility to its clients' enterprisewide issues than those working within respective silos at the client. This can create opportunities to be involved in larger purchasing processes earlier, with a greater chance to influence the scope and scale of the purchase in the marketer's favor.

What does the process look like?

Account Based Marketing thrives on clear prioritization—knowing that levels of effort and opportunity are clearly aligned. What makes it succeed, ultimately, is measurement. Step by step, it looks like this:

01. Measure the whales—prioritize your high-value accounts:

Gain a clear view of the numbers and potential around each existing account. How much revenue does each generate? How much revenue could each potentially generate if you had 100% of their business? What would closing that gap look like in real dollars? What are the odds you can win, and what are the barriers that would prevent you from winning 100% of that business? What are the short-term and long-term prognoses for the industries in which those accounts exist? Ultimately, you want to get to an assumption or index rating of potential revenue you can use to choose which accounts represent the greatest incremental growth opportunity and, therefore, merit dedicated teams. This evaluation should continue, year to year.

02. Feed the baby whales:

Scour your markets for the up-and-coming challengers—those smaller companies that exhibit the same traits as your whales and are pre-positioned to be the next whales. Choose which, if any, merit dedicated effort—only if you assume they represent greater long-term revenue potential than an already established company.

03. Identify the key players:

Just as you have key accounts, each account has key players. Knowing whom to target within an account can enhance your ability to personalize marketing and sales tactics and increase your relevance.

04. Create personalized messaging:

Once you know exactly to whom you need to speak, infuse your campaigns, content, messaging and presentations with the voice of your client. Speak to their pain points and opportunities first and your features and benefits last. Create proactive recommendations for how you can strengthen their existing business or help them uncover new opportunities.

05. Measure and optimize:

Increased personalization and customization should mean increased opportunity evaluation and adjustment. It's no longer about knowing what media mix or messaging works generally to sell your offering but what specifically moves the KPI needle within a specific account or even down to a specific buyer.

06. Continue to build relationships post-sale:

Once your account becomes a client, Account-Based Marketing isn't over. Continue to follow up post-sale to make sure your product has been adapted and delivers on all previous conversations. This is your opportunity to address any questions and to ensure that buyer's remorse doesn't set in. Hopefully, at this point, you'll have a brand advocate—someone who will continue to purchase your product.

So, how do you know if ABM is right for your business?

Account-Based Marketing is not a universal approach for all businesses. It makes sense for companies with multiple services or products that could sell into a variety of departments or business units within a single account. It makes sense for businesses that may be able to provide a more competitive offering through bundling.

Most importantly, it only makes sense when the company's clients are structured in a way that makes it more efficient and advantageous for them to deal with a unified account team on the vendor side. Sometimes, there is a shower-curtain-ring buyer who only needs to get the best price from guys like Del.

Make a pros-and-cons list for using ABM as the sales and service framework for your business.

Walk through the six steps listed in the "transformation from vendor to partner" section above and document your findings.

Download a printable PDF of all notes pages at magnani.com/book

DAY 18

Grab your SEM by the long tail.

AdWords, the original name of Google's advertising platform, belies an implicit bias in the ecosystem.

Words. Not ideas. Not questions. Or answers. Words drive business. Quick connections between concepts and brands. If you're a personal-injury attorney, you want to have your ad appear every time a searcher types "workers compensation" into the search box.

The problem with simplified conceptual connections like this is that there are innumerable reasons that someone may be searching that term—from looking to purchase insurance coverage to wanting clarification on what qualifies for payment, how long one can usually string out workers' compensation payments, or wondering what some generic workers get paid, on average.

And from the advertiser side, when associating with such simplistic terms, there are as many or more business types who may wish to be associated with the term—again, insurance brokers and agents, third-party claims administrators, and other personal-injury attorneys. In the end, it's a noisy and confused information market with low hit rates and generally low returns for most parties involved, with the exception of Google. Yay, AdWords!

Stop thinking "words" and start thinking "answers."

That isn't to say that there is no place for targeting broad, conceptually simplistic terms in your AdWords strategy—especially if you're selling in a commodity market. But if you're attempting to use your SEM to sell a more unique product or service, there is an alternative approach that could deliver a more engaged customer—long-tail SEM.

The long-tail SEM approach is all about understanding what contextually drives customers' search behavior and fulfillment scenarios. Understanding what questions they're trying to answer—what literal and figurative barriers they're trying to overcome—and using that understanding to align a greater portion of the SEM ad budget with those long-tail searches.

Let's go back to the hypothetical personal-injury attorney. Buying an ad against the term "workers' compensation" would place the attorney in front of a far larger set of consumers—but most of those are probably not seeking their offering. Now imagine the attorney creates an AdWords campaign against the term "personal-injury lawyer [pick your city/state/country]." We can see the chances of getting an ad in front of a potential client have increased dramatically. But the attorney is still positioned as a commodity among personal-injury attorneys.

Align SEM campaigns with search terms that enhance your positioning.

Now let's assume the aforementioned attorney is actually a specialist in winning cases that involve lower-back pain. Creating a campaign against the search "best personal injury lawyer lower back cases Chicago" reveals there is no competition for the ad and that it would place them as the only paid ad at the top of the results. There are firms that have done SEO around the idea, but they have not purchased ads.

You'll need a lot more landing pages—with forms.

Search ads are just the first step in presenting a solution or solving a customer need. You need to get them to convert. Now, that could mean downloading something, registering, or, preferably, filling out a form or picking up the phone.

The more specific the issue you create an AdWords campaign around, the greater the need to create dedicated landing pages that present the solution to the users' original search terms and/or the intrinsic promise of the SEM ad itself. Let's assume our hypothetical attorney actually does more than lower-back-pain cases. In fact, the attorney has a healthy practice litigating cases involving commercial trucking accidents. If the attorney creates campaigns around each practice area, there should be a specific landing page tied to each ad.

As a rule of thumb, the less a customer has to hunt for relevance, the greater the average time on the site and the greater the conversion rate. Adding contact forms directly on the landing pages can also increase conversions. Again, it's about minimizing the steps required by a potential customer to get relevant information and connect with the company.

Now seal the deal—optimize for conversions.

Also critical for maximizing effectiveness of the long-tail SEM is conversion rate optimization (CRO). CRO is a process of using analytics and user feedback to improve specific performance metrics of the page. It can mean making adjustments to your UX or design, adding social appeals (awards, client testimonials), or changing the language involved to make conversion methods so it's more obvious and appealing to users. In addition to helping enhance results on key performance indicators (KPIs), CRO should improve ROI on SEM efforts. How's that for a buffet of acronyms?

You'll have to leave "easy" to less successful competitors.

Without question, adopting a long-tail SEM strategy requires more work. You need to gain a more nuanced understanding of your customers' needs and their search habits, and that could mean conducting or auditing primary or secondary research. You need to create and manage a greater number of AdWords campaigns. You need dedicated landing pages for each campaign that are continually reviewed and optimized for driving your conversion metric of choice. But, for all of that effort, you should see a much higher percentage of relevant traffic from your campaigns and a much higher chance of converting that traffic to a customer transaction.

BONUS TOPIC!

B2B SEM 101

There are mountains of information on SEM strategy and getting an AdWords campaign started for B2C and e-commerce products, but B2B, technical, and niche markets have been seriously neglected. Without thousands of people searching for your products every month, a different SEM strategy is needed to be successful.

How many keywords should I have?

The best SEM strategy here is to start small and plan to grow. It's easy for your keyword list to start multiplying out of hand once you add in variations for locations, customer categories, and product options. It's best to start with a short list of distinct keywords, 5–10, that you can use to see which work best. During the first few weeks, you'll want to make updates based on their performance, which is much easier to manage with a small list. (If your list has a couple dozen or more keywords, it might make sense to split them into multiple ad groups—AdWords has some tips on when to use additional ad groups.)

How specific should my keywords be?

AdWords is all about experimenting to see what works best, so try testing both specific and broad keywords.

Specific keywords have several words and describe your exact product or company (e.g., high strength steel processing Chicago).

PROS	CONS
• Highly relevant ads • Lower Cost	• Lower number of searches

One of the biggest differences in SEM strategy for niche markets is how detailed the keywords are. Typically, more-specific keywords are better, but having keywords that are too specific results in having no monthly searches and no one seeing your ads.

Broad keywords are the high-level product categories or business types (e.g., steel processing).

PROS	CONS
• Larger audience • Ads seen earlier • More data	• Higher cost

The trick to running a successful SEM campaign is casting a wide net with broad keywords. The benefits of starting broad certainly outweigh the money that you might spend on irrelevant clicks. The biggest benefit to starting broad is that you'll get valuable data on what your customers are actually searching for. Most of the time, searchers start with a broad search and only get more specific when they get unrelated results. Serving your ads during that first search is your best shot at gaining brand awareness and possibly getting your foot in the door with a potential customer.

How can I prevent irrelevant clicks from eating up my budget?

Negative keywords stop ads from being shown when certain keywords are used. For example, if you don't process stainless steel and you don't serve Canada, "stainless" and "Canada" would prevent those searches from seeing your ads.

Automated rules are another option, as they can limit the amount you spend on a keyword that you think might be too broad by setting monthly or weekly limits to make sure that one keyword doesn't run away with your budget.

How do I know if my keywords are too specific?

The AdWords Keywords Planning Tool[20] lets you see an estimate of monthly searches for a list of keywords you're considering. This is how you determine if you have specific or broad keywords. If you end up with results that have few or no monthly searches, you'll want to take out an adjective or two or throw in some broader product category terms until you see some higher average monthly searches. This will help to even out your SEM strategy.

Keep in mind that this is only an estimate of the keywords that Google has in its database. Don't cross highly relevant keywords off your list just because there's no estimated search volume; these could just be niche enough to not make it into AdWords' database of keywords. Adding keywords with very low search volume won't hurt your account, but the more you have, the more work it'll be to manage the account.

[20] https://ads.google.com/home/tools/keyword-planner/

Should I bid on my own brand?

Even if you're already the top organic result when you search for your own company or brand, here are some of the benefits of adding them as specific keywords:

Credibility

Ads in the search results allow your links to look more professional and more likely to be from a reputable company.

Real Estate

Organic results give four lines of text, but ads with all of the extension features take up twice the space.

Customized Messaging

Ads allow you to deliver your best marketing messaging right in the results page.

Cost

Few people, if any, are bidding on your brand names, so you're able to get better messaging at a lower cost than the rest of your ads.

Competition

If someone else is thinking about bidding on your brand, they'll see higher bid amounts if you're already using them.

This should help you get started with your SEM strategy and avoid some of the pitfalls of advertising in a niche market. Running an effective AdWords campaign of any size is all about testing out new ideas and adjusting based on the data you receive. With a little more patience and an understanding of how to market to a narrow audience, you'll be able to get your messaging out, making you easier to be found by your hard-to-find customers.

What are the most common long-tail searches that drive visitors to your site?

**Craft an SEM ad that explicitly supports your market positioning.
Here are the ad parts you need to draft:**

Short headline:
25 characters max, may appear by itself or with the description

---

Long headline:
90 characters max, may appear by itself or with the description but never with the short headline

---

Description:
90 charters max, only appears with a headline and may be shortened in tight spaces

---

Using the character/length constraints above, draft an SEM ad for each of your top three most important keywords/search phrases?

Download a printable PDF of all notes pages at magnani.com/book

DAY 19

Take the Taylor Swift agency relationship test.

Picking an agency partner?
You should like them "more than a friend."

As with any business relationship, to be successful, the client-agency partnership depends on both parties establishing and delivering against a mutually agreeable set of performance expectations. However, the agency search process and eventual hiring of an agency—strategic, branding, creative, digital, social, etc.— feel more like finding a spouse, without the luxury of a courtship.

Unfortunately, the true expectations of the client, and understanding which expectations matter most, are often left out of the discussion. While every client-agency relationship has its own idiosyncrasies, it has been our experience that if you ask the following five questions—and like the answers you get back—you will have a far better understanding of whether, as Taylor Swift would say, "... it's gonna be forever/Or, it's gonna go down in flames."

Q1: Will I ever see you again?

The flip side of this question is "Who will really work on my account?" It is not uncommon for an agency to have a dedicated pitch team. There is nothing wrong with that as long as you recognize that a good portion of the people you're meeting during the pitch phase is unlikely to work on your account in the future. You have every right to ask about the level of experience and the number of agency team members who will be directly involved in your day-to-day business. You can and should ask how the agency's accounts or projects of similar size and scope to yours are staffed and how that may change over time. Not every project warrants, or has the budget for, the highest level of talent, but you deserve to know exactly what and whom your budget dollars cover.

Q2: What kind of commitment are we talking about?

Speaking of budgets, structuring compensation has historically been one of the most confusing aspects of client-agency relationships. Project-based billing? Retainer? Mixed? Choosing the wrong structure can cause a lot of unnecessary animus on both sides. The simplest structure is fee-for-project, which is a fixed-bid price for a predetermined scope of deliverables. Everyone knows what they start and walk away with, assuming the project follows the initial scope. An hours-based retainer is only slightly more complicated. The client commits to a minimum number of labor hours each month and pays for those hours upfront. At the end of the month, any discrepancies between the hours paid for and the hours consumed are usually reconciled. A mixed project/retainer structure can be the most cost efficient for multi-project, longer-term engagements, but it requires the most reporting and reviewing. There is no "right" way to structure an agreement. A good agency will work with you to create just about any equitable structure you require. Asking a lot of questions about your options upfront and about the level of detail the agency is prepared to provide will go a long way toward building and maintaining a transparent, healthy, and lasting partnership with your agency.

Q3: How will I know this is working?

Gone are the days when any marketer could get away with saying things like "You can't measure that, it's an awareness thing." Everything is measurable, given the proper preparation, implementation and time frame. Ask any potential agency partner what tools and methods they employ to measure success. Their answer should require some input from you on what measures are important to your strategy—awareness, conversions, page rank, social likes and shares, and so on. In general, your agency should be able to offer you a variety of tools and methods for evaluating and reporting on success, whether measuring a long-term strategy or a single tactic.

Q4: Would you mind if I see other people?

Marketing in our current communications environment is complex. Executing well across the spectrum of connection points increasingly requires drawing on a variety of specialized talents and expertise. While digital agencies can certainly provide services that support many of these connections, it is unlikely they are the best resource to handle all of them. You should ask any potential agency partner how well they play in the sandbox. Ask about their experience working on cross-vendor teams for their other clients, what worked well, and what could have worked better. Listen for how they characterize moments of conflict and resolution; it will tell you a lot about how they'll fit into any team you're building.

Q5: What should I be worried about?

Experience with your business or industry is likely table stakes for any agency you're evaluating. When you ask them if they know your business, most could honestly say "yes." However, that doesn't mean they're thinking about your business, your industry, or how it will be affected by market conditions or technological change going forward. Asking the agency what you should be worried about could reveal their nuanced understanding or foresight about your industry, your competitive landscape, and your challenges.

"You love the game."

Of course, this is not the be-all and end-all question set for your agency partner search, but they go a long way toward avoiding an agency nightmare dressed like a daydream.

For use in your next agency review: Rewrite the above questions in terms more specific or applicable to your business.

DAY
20

Learn to read the tea leaves.

Innovate. **Activate.** Accelerate.

On dashboards and divination.

Harry Potter and Ron Weasley sit in their very first divination class. Today, Professor Trelawney is instructing the class on the mysterious practice of reading tea leaves. At the request of the professor, Ron makes a poor attempt to read meaning from the dregs at the bottom of Harry's teacup.

"Well," Ron mutters, "Harry's got a sort of a … uh, wonky cross and that's trials and suffering, and that there … that could be the sun, and that's happiness. So, you're gonna suffer … but, you're gonna be happy about it?"

"Give me the cup," demands Professor Trelawney. She quickly takes hold of the cup, glances at the bottom, immediately gasps and drops the cup. "My b-boy," she ominously stutters. "My dear … you have the Grim."

And that, my friends, sounds like a web analytics project.

Two people … same set of data … wildly different interpretations. The novice peers at the cup and sees a series of interconnected, but contradictory, patterns, thereby delivering a nonsensical prediction of future activities. The expert gazes into the dregs and reads an entirely different (and, more importantly, a far deeper) meaning, with greater implications for how one should move through the future.

First, a caveat: I am in no way saying that web analytics are magic. In fact, when done properly, it's a highly scientific process requiring hypotheses and experiments to measure the veracity of those hypotheses against the data we collect.

Web analytics are a wonderful thing. They allow us to see how our marketing programs and web properties are performing in the real world, with actual customers. But, by their very nature, the data we collect from our web properties are measures of the past.

How can we use the past to make better predictions against the future? Better yet, how can we structure our dashboards to provider a deeper reading of our customers' digital activities … and how can we tie those activities to the measures that directly affect the bottom line of our business?

Hop on your broomsticks and follow me.

Begin with the macro.

The real failure in most analytics reporting isn't that the reporting or the cursory evaluation of the metrics is wrong. Yes, it's important to know how many people visited your website last week, what they looked at and what they did. The larger issue lies in not linking the micro-metrics (visitors, time on page, etc.) to macro-metrics (business goals). If, for example, you haven't identified the relationship between the number of unique sessions on your landing page and the overall sales goals for your company for the year, you're a) wasting your time in putting the report together and b) not supplying meaningful data to the people who need to make decisions based on those metrics.

While developing a dashboard (and the activities that are represented by that dashboard), start with what you know. In any organization, most employees should know the business goals for the year. Is your organization targeting increased revenue? Increased profit? New users? Lower call-center volume? What's that magic number?

Now, evaluate the program you're thinking of implementing. Does that program help any of those numbers? How? What specifically will your program do to move that magic number in a direction your C-suite would approve? Do you have the answer to that question, yet? Yes? Super. That's the metric your whole dashboard (heck, your whole program) is centered around.

Next, focus on the micro.

Once the macro-metrics are identified, examine the micro-metrics available to you. These are going to be the standard analytics often seen populating dashboards. Some examples may include sessions, users, page views, bounce rate, etc. Think of these numbers as the raw materials of our dashboard. They have a direct correlation to our customers' activities in the real world and most directly reflect the success or failure of a particular campaign or initiative. Identify which micro-metrics (or what combinations) marry best to the activities you're wishing to encourage during your campaign.

But how can we determine that activities measured by our micro-metrics correlate with the large macro-metrics? This is where experience and creativity begin to play greater influence.

Jump the gap.

In most organizations, the keeper of the macro-metrics sits apart from the keeper of the micro-metrics (i.e., the CFO may not even know the name of the analytics manager). This is both common and unfortunate. Unfortunate in that the CFO might be pleasantly surprised by a spike in sales at the same time the analytics manager might be pleasantly surprised by a spike in web traffic, which comes as no surprise to the marketing manager who has been busting her hump for the past two months working on a well-crafted, well-designed, action-oriented paid-media campaign. But our marketing manager has no idea that her actions had a direct reflection on the sales numbers because that information is kept behind a wall.

So, how do we change this? Shocker ... it's going to require communication. First identify the keeper of the information you need to inform the success or failure of your campaigns. Then, become best friends with that person. What's his or her favorite coffee drink? How many pets does he/she have? And the names of those pets? Set a standing meeting. Have a phone call once a week to discuss the high-level macro-metrics. You need to jump that gap between what you know (the micro-metrics) and what you may not be privy to (the macro-metrics).

Now take the information you know exists and structure your dashboard around it. Roughly, your dashboard should start with the broadest information on the first page and get increasingly granular as you move through it. Additionally, you may consider creating custom metrics that help demonstrate a helpful correlation between micro- and macro-metrics. Custom metrics add value by providing insight into the overall trends in your data, instead of merely the point-in-time perspective that many dashboards stop at.

Read the tea leaves.

The real expertise in evaluating metrics lies not in viewing the numbers ... it's in understanding how the numbers reflect actions real people took in the real world and how that activity helped or hurt your campaign. Attempt to see the unseen. And this requires two skills: the empathy to understand the how and why of your customers and the ability to draw a story from their actions as expressed in the metrics. And, not surprisingly, developing those skills requires repetition and reflection.

In closing, the more we attempt to look through the numbers and relate them to the larger stories of the businesses and clients we work for, the greater value we'll inject into our dashboards to provide real, actionable information our teams can use. In telling those stories, we'll be less Ron Weasley and more Professor Trelawney.

Create a two-column list:

Column 1:

List the analytics measures your business is tracking.

Column 2:

List measurable business outcomes associated with each measure.

_____

_____

_____

_____

_____

_____

_____

_____

_____

_____

_____

_____

_____

_____

_____

_____

_____

_____

_____

_____

_____

Schedule a standing call or meeting with whoever in your company is keeper of the analytics.

Download a printable PDF of all notes pages at magnani.com/book

DAY
21

Don't overdose on the good stuff.

Can you do too much of a good thing?

There is a phrase in medicine: "the poison is in the dose," meaning, that no substance is inherently beneficial or dangerous, you just need to mind the amount administered. Humans need things like vitamin A and water but ingest too much of either, and they'll make you ill, or worse yet, dead. Perhaps, unsurprisingly, the same can be said of today's technology-driven marketing practices. Here are five things really smart marketers do to remain successful that, if overdone, could actually impede the success of your plans.

Five ways smart marketing can go too far.

01. Increasing the level of detail in your analytics.

As marketers, we have an unprecedented level of analytics available to us. So, when given the option, why not increase your effectiveness by enhancing the level of analytical detail you collect? Before you answer, first ask yourself the following questions:

- **Are you really only substituting increased volume for insight?**
  Most businesses are not taking full advantage of the data they already have.

- **Have you fully detailed and examined the story your current data and analytics are telling you?**
  Collecting data is one thing, but the actual implications of the data are where many businesses fall short.

- **What insights do your current metrics provide?**
  What will you do with additional measurement and how will it impact, or change, your current marketing strategies and behaviors? Is the cost of the additional analytics offset by the potential gains it will provide in sales or other KPIs?

  So, what should you do? The truth, for most resource-constrained businesses, is that it's better to narrow the data points you review to only those that are most important to improving business KPIs (key performance indicators). Then prioritize your time and resources, optimizing your user experience around those conversion behaviors that drive those KPIs.

02. Focusing on your best customers.

There has never been a marketer with unlimited time and unlimited money. Resources are always constrained (Geico's seemingly unlimited television commercial budget notwithstanding). That's why, as preached in every marketing or business school, the sound strategy is to focus your efforts on maintaining and maximizing relationships with your best customers.

It's the lowest-risk way to see a positive return on your investment. That is still true. But often, focus turns into exclusivity. What many marketers forget is that when they manage risk down to zero, they will also be managing potential opportunities to zero.

What should you do? The best way to catalyze new opportunities may be allocating a percentage of your marketing budget for experimentation. Test your hunches. Take creative risks. Look for untapped new audiences. But only if you're committed to systematically measuring and analyzing the results!

03. Going all-in on a mobile-first strategy.

While more than 50% of B2B and B2C transactions begin or involve mobile experiences—despite what most marketing publications may be preaching, for most B2B (and some B2C) marketers—it's too soon to abandon or give short shrift to the desktop. What should you do? Well, the simple answer is, support both platforms. Ensure your web experience is fully responsive and offers equal ability to facilitate any and all conversions.

The more complex approach is to scour your analytics to fully understand the differences in user behavior across and between platforms. Break down your user flows on each device type into micro-transactions (making sure you implement corresponding hooks in your analytics) to better understand what UX/UI features/moments in the mobile or desktop experiences are enhancing or depressing your overall conversion rates. Then continue to optimize those micro-transactions by platform against your conversion goals. And, of course, continue to monitor ongoing changes in share of user sessions by platform and allocate future development budgets and resources based on your users' rate of mobile adoption.

04. Maximizing engagement with customers on social media.

Where once most marketers used the number of followers as the preeminent measure of a successful social strategy, lately there has been more emphasis on engagement numbers. While both are decent enough measures of activity, they are not proven, in and of themselves, to be drivers of ROI. Further, raw engagement numbers don't necessarily convey sentiment. And finally, focusing on quantity of engagements versus quality can impart noise into your channels as well as muddy the intended message within each channel.

What should you do? Like most points made here, we suggest thinking first about optimizing or maximizing conversions or behaviors that drive business KPIs. Spend most of your time engaging in conversations that support those goals and metrics. Make all posts and conversations actionable— always try to provide links to conversion points, etc. Perhaps base success not on how many people saw or "liked" your posts but on how many became actively engaged in a behavior you want to drive.

05. Expanding your content library.

It seems the majority of B2B marketers have all jumped onto the content train. The idea was that white papers, blog posts and articles are more trusted media (versus banner ads or direct marketing), so they would more easily capture attention and pull in more interested customers while they are at their most engaged—researching a given topic. While there is certainly an SEO benefit to adding a greater volume of relevant content to your site, most B2B content is never experienced by the intended audience. Creating good, useful content is time- and resource-intensive. And unless that content is actively engaged with by users, it will not provide the desired lift in online engagement or conversions. In other words, generating content for content's sake equals time and resources wasted.

What should you do? First, understand that more is not better. Better is better. What does that mean? Well, when creating your next piece of content, evaluate if what you're saying is uniquely valuable to your audience. Ask yourself:

1. Are you providing insights, ideas or factual information that aren't available already in multiple places?

2. Is there an audience waiting for content on the topic? Is it really thought leadership, or simply "me too" SEO fodder?

3. Does the new content present a previously unknown opportunity for action?

4. Will the content you're creating actively support your strategic business goals?

5. And, most importantly, what target segments, specifically, will benefit from engaging with the content?

If you can answer all of those questions and still think that producing the content is worth your limited time and resources (as well as the time and resources your customers will expend consuming it), then create it, push it out and promote it like mad.

The short version:

Do everything in the right amount, for the right reasons!

Write down which, if any, of the above excesses your business is guilty of.
Under each offense, list three issues/items you could address.

Download a printable PDF of all notes pages at magnani.com/book

DAY 22

Up your millennials game.

How do you market to millennials?

Over the past few years, whether from existing or potential clients, some variation of the following question has been posed: "What do we have to do to attract more millennials?" First step, in our experience, is to understand why any difference in approach might be required.

First, some background.

For previous generations, in the U.S. at least, characteristics like affiliation or membership defined status. That could be illustrated in a number of ways. What school you attended. What clubs you belonged to. At what company you chose to spend your career. Hence, affiliation had inherent value of its own. As Generation X came of age, possessions defined status and the social currency was the outward signaling of that ability to consume. McMansions. A BMW. Branded clothing, e.g., Polo, IZOD®, Hilfiger®.

But as millennials came of age, the security once offered by corporations was a historical relic and the traditional economic safe harbors (e.g., housing, bonds, etc.) were in collapse, threatening to take down the global economy.

The assumption that traditional institutions, including corporations or large public institutions, would be around to take care of them in any way seemed imaginary. And ostentatious symbolic consumerism, once embraced by previous generations, seemed hollow.

The generational shift in cultural currency.

Given the circumstances, it was unsurprising that out of this emerged a trend among millennials to put less value in institutions or material possessions and, by proxy, less value in the social status afforded by them.

Further, millennials who attended college, more so than any previous generation, were confronted with higher debt levels and fewer job prospects. And, as mentioned earlier, the feeling remained that once they acquired a position, there were no guarantees those jobs would remain in place, regardless of their performance.

The long term became wildly unpredictable. Which led to an entirely predictable cultural reflex of assigning greater social value to experiences. The future could take away a house, but it could never take memories or past experiences.

And, finally, came the rise of social media as a ubiquitous marketplace upon which those experiences could be showcased and their inherent value determined by an open exchange of "likes" and "re-shares," which made gaining status from photos of a trip to Bhutan more compelling than posting the earning of a new professional certification. So, what's a marketer to do to appeal to this generation?

Elevate the individual experiences.

If affiliation with a brand, in and of itself, holds little incremental value to millennials, brands will need to improve on delivering something that does—experiences.

Take, for example, a B2B company seeking a rise in connections with millennial-aged buyers at a trade show. Where once a basic beer-and-wine reception in a hotel ballroom would have sufficed for a networking event, to successfully compete for free time today, the company may have to plan something more like a behind-the-scenes evening tour at a local craft brewery. And food and beverage choices now require sensitivities to a variety of dietary schools of thought, from vegan to paleo to gluten-free.

This first generation of "digital natives" has grown accustomed to continuously improving, technology-facilitated customer experiences. You had better serve up a totally friction-free shopping experience. Millennials are not going to wait around to complete an overly onerous checkout process. And that attitude extends to every transaction.

Millennials cannot understand why anyone would put up with having to stand on a street corner, hand in the air, waiting for a cab to pass by—they open Uber on their phones. They don't head to nytimes.com for news—it appears constantly in their Facebook, Snapchat and Instagram feeds. And more than 50% of millennials cite their smartphone as their primary and only personal computing device. They won't sit down to consume content—they'll multitask and graze on information as they go through their day.

Given that, it's not surprising millennials generally will not take it upon themselves to slog through an arduously designed web experience or overly long editorial content. They expect providers not to serve up information but to give them control over that experience. Therefore, modernization of web experiences (e.g., mobile-first design, more short-form content, social integration, personalization) will be paramount in establishing and maintaining ongoing online connections with millennials.

Create opportunities to form relationships.

Millennials can exhibit a tendency to approach building relationships with greater caution. On the flip side, they're open to making themselves more available online. Marketers can capitalize on both of these tendencies by creating more robust tools for online interaction and community building around the brand, e.g., user forums, communal hashtags, etc. In categories with a large number of avid consumers, they'll gladly add to the conversation, as long as users feel they have sufficient controls over privacy and levels of sharing.

Reward participation.

Seventy-six percent of millennials have joined some form of loyalty program. That is a much higher level of participation than their parents' generation. However, they expect those programs to be free, easy, and fast. Associations could leverage that behavior by rewarding members with points for participating in, recommending, or growing the member community. Points could potentially be used for reduced fees or VIP experiences at events.

Emphasize your greater social good.

A third of millennials will choose or abandon a brand based solely on causes. And nearly two-thirds place high loyalty value on brands that engage in causes, philanthropy, or endeavors that reflect their beliefs/values. Therefore, it's fair to assume brands that can effectively communicate their greater social value, both among their existing customers and the general population, will have a greater chance of attracting brand evangelists and maintaining loyalty among millennials.

When in doubt, ask.

Whether you're focused on creating or delivering content, increasing the value of a transaction, or creating new online experiences, perhaps the most valuable activity in the development process is engaging and understanding customers. Engage the market through focus groups, ethnographic studies, one-on-one interviews, or surveys. Get an understanding about what your company or brand does well, what you could do better, or what customers value most about their relationship with you.

Or, just treat them like everyone else.

Often, the generational affiliations used by marketers as a predictor for behavioral or purchasing habits, when focused on too precisely, can greatly miss the mark. In some markets, the smartest and most efficient segmentation is generationally agnostic. Increasingly, due to the wilds of the internet, an increasing percentage of cultural references are shared among chronologically separated cohorts. Consequently, we can use technology and big data to define consumer groups that are similarly culture-hungry, up to date, and better identified by their behavioral and psychographic similarities than by their age.

Consider and write down five ways the emerging millennial workforce may change your markets.

What three things should your business be doing differently given the above considerations?

Download a printable PDF of all notes pages at magnani.com/book

DAY 23

Meet Generation Z.

Meet the largest generational population. Now market to them.

At 26% of the overall population, Generation Z (born 1996–2012) is poised to wield massive influence on markets for the foreseeable future. While there is still much unknown about how this group will behave once they enter the workforce, en masse, there are already some interesting behavioral differences emerging that all marketers should understand.

Five Things You Should Understand About Generation Z

01. Mobile isn't cool. It's life.

A study[21] showed that while only 4% of millennials and older believe 13 is an appropriate age for owning a smartphone, 18% of Generation Z members think it is. One might attribute this to youthful hubris, but the fact is that this generation has never known a time without "iDevices." They see mobile handsets and constant connectivity as integral to life, resulting in 98% owning smartphones and devoting an average of 3.5 hours per day to its[22] use.

02. It's not an 8-second attention span; it's instant prioritization.

Much ado has been made about the declining attention span of Generation Z[23]. Reports cite research claiming that since 2000, teenage attention spans have decreased from somewhere around the millennials' 11 seconds to Generation Z's 8 seconds. But I think using that number as any indication of a decline in cognitive ability is misleading.

When viewed in the context of the exponential acceleration of data being created, posted and shared, combined with a proliferation of screens, it would seem that there would be an increasing need to be able to instantaneously evaluate individual data points and summarily dismiss or elevate their importance to "full attention." It's not that they cannot pay attention, necessarily, but that having any meaningful interactions with incoming stimuli requires a highly developed ability to triage in real time.

If you're a marketer, be forewarned. This emerging consumer juggernaut hates anything perceived as an ad and has an amazing ability to filter out any marketing less than 100% relevant to them.

[21] http://genhq.com/wp-content/uploads/2016/01/iGen-Gen-Z-Tech-Disruption-Research-White-Paper-c-2016-Center-for-Generational-Kinetics.pdf)
[22] https://blog.globalwebindex.com/chart-of-the-day/gen-z-spending-3-5-hours-mobiles-daily/
[23] https://www.bloomberg.com/opinion/articles/2014-06-18/nailing-generation-z

03. Optimism is baked right in.

A 2016 survey[24] conducted by Lincoln Financial Group paints a picture of a generation far more optimistic than the preceding generation, the millennials. Further, they are more aware of and focused on planning for their financial futures. Of course, only 33% of Generation Z have even reached college age, so that could change. But as of today, 50% of Gen Zers think America is headed in the right direction, versus 42% of millennials or 34% of Gen Xers. And 51% of Gen Zers believe that the American Dream "still holds true."

Sixty-four percent of Gen Zers have already started researching or talking to others about their financial futures and, on average, they begin those conversations by age 13. And after starting those conversations, 95% of those Gen Z planners feel optimistic about their future, in general, and 93% feel optimistic about their financial futures, specifically. An extension of that thinking, Generation Z has attitudes toward savings that rival even the Depression-era Traditionalists. More than 71% think savings are important.

04. Social influencers are the new celebrities.

Gen Z is more likely to watch hours of YouTube[25] than television. In fact, 63% say they prefer to see real people than celebs in their ads. Though, to be fair, they consider the Kardashians among those "real" people. This fact should point those marketers toward a strategy of supporting a stable of niche promoters rather than placing all of their marketing eggs into a single celebrity basket.

05. They prefer convenience over brands.

Research from Accenture[26] about the purchasing behaviors of Gen Zers is likely to excite Silicon Valley venture capitalists and terrify traditional e-retailers. It points to a near-universal desire for technology-driven, cutting-edge shopping experiences like "instant" one-hour delivery, in-store kiosks and voice-activated shopping. And they have a commensurate appetite for switching retailers based on which provide the greater of those experiences.

Further, they make shopping social. They consult family and friends for insights and opinions on products in real time while shopping. They leave reviews and can be unapologetic about giving retailers feedback. And, following that, they are twice as likely to consult YouTube before making a purchase (see item #4, above). Worse yet for traditional retailers, Gen Zers raised in the sharing economy have little issue renting fashion items, furnishings, home goods, and even appliances.

[24] https://newsroom.lfg.com/sites/lfg.newshq.businesswire.com/files/doc_library/file/FINAL_Gen_Z_Sourced_Deck_8.9.16.pdf
[25] https://www.forbes.com/sites/rachelarthur/2016/03/16/generation-z/#66270322909
[26] https://www.accenture.com/t20170210T012359__w__/us-en/_acnmedia/PDF-44/Accenture-Retail-Customer-Research-Executive-Summary-2017.pdf

This is not the last word.

It's a good bet that anyone over the age of 25 can tell you how differently they view their world, their careers, and their social groups today versus how they may have in their mid or late teens. So, it's yet to be seen how this growing and increasingly influential population group we're calling Generation Z will shake out emotionally, professionally, or as consumers. In any case, their influence is sure to be massive, and it's time for all marketers to start paying attention.

Want to learn more about Gen Z?

Magnani conducted proprietary research in order to help inform the innovation process for products, services, and technologies targeting this up-and-coming generation, as well as to gain a better understanding of the customer experiences they'll demand and their communication preferences. Check out our full Gen Z report: https://www.magnani.com/gen-z-report[27].

[27] https://www.magnani.com/gen-z-report

What could you be doing more of to generate affinity and brand preference among Gen Zers?

What should you be doing less of?

_____

_____

_____

_____

_____

_____

_____

_____

_____

_____

_____

_____

_____

_____

_____

_____

_____

_____

_____

_____

_____

_____

Download the complete Gen Z research report:

https://www.magnani.com/gen-z-report

Download a printable PDF of all notes pages at magnani.com/book

ACCELERATE.

" You don't have to swing hard to hit a home run. If you got the timing, it'll go. "

–Yogi Berra

How will you move ahead?

No business has unlimited time or resources. If the previous sections of this book are about choosing what game you're playing, and in what arenas you'll find the best luck, this section is about how you might strategically approach the game itself.

DAY 24

Think like a challenger.

Challenge everything—especially yourself.

The first thing to remember about all successful challenger brands is that what they exist to challenge is not the market leader, per se, but the status quo. From a competitive messaging and positioning standpoint, challenger brands derive power not from comparisons to the leader but from an idea that offers customers an affiliation, experience, or advantage the market leaders do not or cannot offer. And, by doing so, challenger brands avoid price comparisons and command a premium for their offerings. So, how do you know your brand is ready to take up the challenge? Take a moment to consider applying any of the following three challenger brand strategies to your business.

01. Embody a challenger's hero story.

There are three basic character archetypes any challenger brand should fit into. Let's take a look at them and their implications:

The Enabler

This challenger archetype makes an existing product, or service, qualitatively similar to the market leader, but available to a new or different audience. This could mean an offer of parity at a lower price, availability to a new demographic segment, a different geographic location, or all of the above. Think: Apple Computer® (1977), Southwest® Airlines, or Aldi™ food stores.

The Disruptor

This challenger archetype satisfies the same need as the market leader, but through a substantively different experience. That could mean a product substitution, a new distribution method or radically altered service paradigm. Think: Apple® (1996) with the first iPhone, Lemonade Insurance, Amazon®, Airbnb®, and Uber.

The Altruist

This challenger archetype offers a comparatively similar product or service experience to the market leader but enhances the transaction by linking it to some form of community support or social responsibility. Think: Tom's® shoes, Bombas socks, Newman's Own® Foods, BoxLunch™ and (RED)™.

02. Relish your limitations

Challenger brands are always hungry. While every company these days seems to need to accomplish more with less, challenger brands derive some form of defiant energy from the task. If challenger brands were boxers, they would be fighting up a weight class. That is not a sign of hubris but a confident embrace of humility. It's not about pretending to be the champion's size but using its size against it. So, getting beyond metaphors and analogies, what does that mean in real market-planning terms? It means approaching budgeting with clinical precision. It means constantly measuring, analyzing and optimizing every small detail of your marketing and media plans so that every dollar and every effort generates maximum returns. It means embracing a narrower positioning that can be more readily communicated and capitalized upon and a more focused approach to media planning. Ultimately, it means having the discipline to engage in only those activities and opportunities that support your strategy—and loving it.

03. Indulge an appetite for risk equal to your aspirations.

Any proverbial David will never beat Goliath playing Goliath's game. David only wins by devising a new game altogether. But making that move requires an appetite for entering unknown territories, and taking risks. How much risk? Well, that calculus is always a function of the disparity in resources, awareness, affinity, and scale between challenger and champion, as well as the time frame within which the challenger needs or wants to bridge, or even surmount, those disparities. So, what risks have historically paid off for challenger brands? First, and perhaps most obviously, creative risk. If you can't outsize the champion's media budget, you have to outsize their ideas. There are a number of ways challengers find success in risk taking:

Creative risk:
This requires some form of novelty; breaking through with a unique creative campaign or a bold bet on a new form of media. Successful challengers have also found reward in taking strategic risks in their approach to distribution.

Supply risk:
Limiting inventories or the number of outlets, betting scarcity protects margin.

Affiliation risks:
Estimating exclusivity, or halo effect, of distribution partners can increase desirability.

Channel risk:
Offering a new, previously unavailable, form of distribution. Some challengers take product risks, creating an entirely new means for consumers to satisfy the need the champion does currently.

Ultimately, challenger brands are a powerful mix of discipline and passion.

The truth is, most brands are, in a basic sense, challenger brands—existing in a challenging marketplace, trying to make the most of constrained budgets, limited internal resources, and accelerated expectations for return on investment. Succeeding as a challenger brand, however, requires a higher level of awareness and market insight, a more disciplined approach to planning and prioritization, and a commitment to taking calculated creative and market risks. And the best of the best enjoy every minute of it.

What challenger hero story best aligns with your business strategy and why?

If you focused dollars and efforts more narrowly, what marketing, sales, PR efforts could you enhance or omit to improve your measurable return on budget?

What SKUs could you drop or improve to better align with your strategy?

What about your business would you be willing to risk (market share, relationships with certain distribution partners, etc.) to attain your competitive goals?

Download a printable PDF of all notes pages at magnani.com/book

DAY 25

Rethink your growth strategy.

Growth is rarely accidental.

There are certainly anecdotal examples where businesses or products were unexpectedly discovered by a new market segment and sales grew exponentially, seemingly out of the blue, overnight—Mane 'n Tail® shampoo jumping from an animal care product to the traditional beauty market, or Avon Skin So Soft moisturizing lotion being adopted as insect repellent. But waiting for that kind of magic to happen is not a growth strategy. Creating a successful growth strategy is complicated and the path forward can be, at times, counterintuitive. If you're charged with creating a growth strategy, here are five counterintuitive facts you should consider before finalizing your plans.

Five Counterintuitive Facts about Growth Strategy:

01. You can't hack your way to sustainable growth.

There are myriad articles floating around the internet claiming growth is a few simple "hacks" away. Growth hacking is a term coined in Silicon Valley that encompasses any number of ways to acquire users/customers/accounts with no regard for cost of acquisition, scalability, or sustainability. The driving force behind growth hacking is that, among certain investor communities, the growth itself determines value, not the underlying financial viability of the model. And if your plan is to secure a financial exit prior to the bottom falling out, it's a seemingly logical choice for a budding startup. But enterprise-level businesses that are concerned with creating sustainable and profitable growth should look to more sound analysis and planning and to less fairy dust and magical thinking.

02. You should actually be thinking more short term.

If your business plan is the entire game of chess (five years), your growth plan is more about executing your next few moves (90 days to two years). Your growth strategy needs to be aligned with your business strategy, of course, but they have different objectives. Your business plan may offer a high-level view of how to create a more sustainable and defensible long-term market position, whereas growth planning should remain agile and adjust to fluctuating market conditions like increasing share or achieving specific revenue or profitability goals.

03. Sometimes you grow faster by saying "no."

It's easy to think that growth is simply about selling to more customers. But the truth is, not all customers are equally good for the business. No company has unlimited time and resources. Focusing time and resources against only those customers that can be most easily acquired and contribute most positively to the bottom line can not only improve returns, but it can also have an accelerating effect by signaling and clarifying market positioning to distribution partners and customers, alike.

04. It's nearly impossible to grow sustainably by reducing price.

Frequently, businesses will effectively buy market share through price reductions. The thinking usually goes, "If we cut the price 5%, and we get a 10% increase in sales, the reduction has more than paid for itself!" But where that reasoning is flawed is the fact that most businesses operate at profit margins of less than 10% of sales. In this case, assuming the theoretical company has a normal operating margin of 10%, if you reduce the price 5%, you actually need to double sales (using no additional manpower or resources) just to realize the same profit in real dollars they were achieving before the price reduction. Sometimes competition will force concessions on price, but it should be your last option.

05. You don't need end goals.

Don't assume this means you shouldn't measure performance. Quite the opposite. But the measures that matter are more about ongoing momentum, direction and acceleration than an end state. Are increases in sales or revenue levels by product or service mix aligning with predictions? Is the number of accounts increasing at the expected rate? Are new customers renewing at an acceptable rate? In other words, are your company behaviors resulting in the ongoing market behaviors you need to maintain the desired growth trajectory?

Ultimately, growth is a process.

So, a final thought for this chapter: While a long-term business strategy can be more of a set-and-forget (the destination of your trip), your growth strategy is more like the ongoing monitoring of your speed, acceleration, RPM, and mileage along the way.

What are the pros and cons of your existing growth strategies?

How do your estimates of growth relate to overall industry/category growth patterns?

What are you doing now that you might rethink, given the above considerations?

Download a printable PDF of all notes pages at magnani.com/book

DAY 26

Distinguish between technology and transformati

Three tips for a successful digital transformation that aren't about technology.

"Digital transformation" seems to be the catchphrase of the decade. More and more, we receive requests from potential new clients asking for assistance with just that. But, as it was with SEO in 2010 or mobile apps in 2012, many of those requesters treat the idea of a digital transformation as something of a one-off effort. A box to be checked. Often a digital property purchased or redesigned. The truth, however, is that when done in a truly transformational way, the process of getting to real transformation is anything but box checking. If you're tasked with leading your company's digital transformation, following these three seemingly counterintuitive tips could dramatically improve your chances of success:

01. Stop using the word digital.

The phrase "digital transformation" implies something separate from the normal business of the company. It's the kind of mental compartmentalization that we find leads to that check-box mentality. Try to substitute more meaningful words in place of "digital"—like, "business," or "customer journey," understanding, of course, any truly transformative change will likely require a digital solution.

A simple reframing like this increases lateral thinking and prompts more substantive conversations. In other words, you stop focusing on how you can improve systems within the business and start asking how you can improve the business itself.

02. Try writing the first draft of your plan without mentioning specific technology.

Technology is a means to an end, not the end itself. And transformation, in and of itself, holds no inherent value for the business. Writing your plan—objectives, strategies, goals, KPIs, timing, expected returns, customer experience benefits, etc.—without listing specific technology implementations forces you to examine and evaluate the business implications on their own merits.

At Magnani, this is part of our Narrative-Based Innovation methodology. We explore and document the expected qualitative and quantitative outcomes of a successful transformation. We create a story about motivations and expectations, not hardware or software. We have found that once you build consensus around what that experience should feel like and deliver, the story can serve, throughout the process, as a touchstone for evaluating and prioritizing proposed technology implementations. Will this technology deliver the experience we outlined in our story as optimal for the business and its customers? How might it compromise that vision? Is any potential trade-off worth it?

03. Try to disrupt your own business.

In an earlier chapter, we outlined three proven paths to disruptive innovation. The point of that chapter applies here. Disruption is imminent. Technology is lowering barriers to entry in every industry. Emerging generations have little tolerance for adapting to cumbersome experiences. They expect and demand better.

If you can envision the most desirable customer experience, technology always finds a way.

If you're charged with plotting your business' path through the digital transformation process, you'd be well served to look beyond the traditional limits of an IT or Marketing Department project. Start by creating a vision for an unsurpassed customer experience, then back your way into the technology. And, ultimately, you should presume succeeding in the challenge might boil down to two main choices: disrupt or be disrupted. We advocate, unreservedly, for the former.

Can you explain the desired outcome of your digital transformation strategy without mentioning any technology?

Download a printable PDF of all notes pages at magnani.com/book

DAY 27

Embrace deep learning.

The wave of automation and AI disruption is coming.

We see new advances in digital automation and artificial intelligence (AI) nearly every day. Much the way industrial robot technology reduced the number of available manufacturing jobs in the U.S. in the 1980s, the combination of digital automation and AI is poised to disrupt virtually every industry at some point in the coming decade. The question is: How can you position your company to be the disruptor, not the disrupted?

People and patterns and predictions, oh my.

Why should you care about deep learning? For marketers, a simple way to think about deep learning is that it's ultimately about presenting customers with exactly what they want, whether or not they know that they want it. That could mean an experience, a bit of information, an ad, or a suggestion for a specific product. But what is deep learning?

Deep learning is a subset of artificial intelligence (AI) derived from the science of neural networks. And neural networks are simply an attempt to mimic the way scientists theorize how our own brains process information and make sense of the world. Basically, a neural network self-optimizes its performance on a desired task based on exposure to structured and unstructured data.

I spy with my AI ...

For example, let's imagine we're creating a deep-learning-based image-recognition system designed to spot a product—a specifically branded can of soda—in photos posted on social media because we'd like to give a shoutout, through our own social accounts, to the poster for their brand loyalty.

The first thing we would need to do is train the deep-learning neural network, using a number of verified positive and negative sources—e.g., photos containing said soda can, pre-tagged as a hit, as well as photos with no can correspondingly tagged as a non-hit. Next, the system would be fed untagged positive and negative photos. The digital patterns in those photos would be compared to whatever digital patterns emerged from reviewing the initial guided positive and negative inputs.

If the system recognizes what it has determined is the pattern for "branded can," it marks that photo as a positive hit. At this stage, the system will require human feedback to determine whether that positive hit was, in fact, positive and whether other photos were falsely tagged as hits or non-hits. Each iteration, every data point, refines the neural network to better identify its proper target. And with data sets that span the internet, you can imagine how refined those algorithms can get.

But here's the interesting part: Humans generally can't read or understand those algorithms. We don't know what criteria the network is using, per se. We only know it's getting better (or worse) at identifying the branded can. And there are plenty of times the technology fails completely, not to mention offensively[28].

How this "portrait" was made

1. Generate random polygons

2. Feed them into a deep-learning, neural-net face detector

3. Mutate to increase recognition confidence until the neural net is reasonably sure it "sees" a face

A synthetic portrait "recognized" among random overlaid polygons by deep learning AI at:
http://iobound.com/pareidoloop/

28 https://www.theguardian.com/technology/2015/may/20/flickr-complaints-offensive-auto-tagging-photos

Marketers love patterns, too.

That ability to recognize patterns is an obvious benefit to marketers. What is segmentation besides recognition of patterns? Demographic patterns. Psychographic patterns. Behavioral patterns. Spending patterns. But where we all used to divine these patterns in a more general and collective fashion across the aggregate population, now powerful deep-learning AI can make continuous, deft pattern-related decisions on an individual by individual basis, thousands of times a second. It can, and it does. Let's take a look at how.

Real-time media targeting and buying.

Gone are the days when media purchasing was planned months in advance. Programmatic media and real-time bidding platforms are using deep-learning AI to assess, in real time, the level of intent or interest a user may have for a product, service, or experience. Again, don't think of this as testing against a static target profile. The system is learning in real time as well, refining its model and iterating—ultimately looking to optimize levels of desired behavior generated (clicks, purchases, etc.) per media dollar spent.

All the while, the system is developing both a detailed predictive model for intent as well as a more accurate program for moving those customers from intent to conversion. This also allows marketers to scale campaigns more precisely as well as increase their ability to track media ROI.

Truly personalized experiences.

All UX designers strive to create as intuitive an experience as possible—minimizing the time and effort required of a user to connect with whatever it is they desire. Deep-learning systems driving those interactions can process the data surrounding users' behaviors. That data obviously can be used to provide suggested actions correlated to the users' past actions.

That could range from something as simple as a "You might also like" shopping moment to something as complicated as proactively making dinner reservations for a customer because you know from the location of their mobile device or credit card activity that they are suddenly in an unfamiliar city and that they enjoy experimenting with more exotic foods while traveling.

So, how can you get started thinking about this?

01. Ask how a competitor using advanced AI could beat you at your own game.

Diagram your complete path to purchase on a whiteboard. Evaluate every part of your business for any moment along that path where automation or AI-facilitated decision-making could reduce process time, costs and user frustrations. Also, look for any part of your path to purchase where customers drop off or fail to convert and try to reimagine those points with AI or automation assistance. Take time to explore emerging technologies that could directly or indirectly affect your market, long term.

Now, look at your market and ask, regardless of organizational, technical or monetary constraints: What would the ideal experience for the majority of your customers look like? What do your customers value/like/dislike about everyone's current offerings?

Finally, get your smartest people—from operations, sales, marketing, admin, et al.—and design your worst competitive nightmare. What special expertise would they offer? What advantages would they have over your business? How would they price? What capital expenditures would they need to build their infrastructure, I.T. or facilities?

02. Figure out what it would take for them to get off the ground.

Once you decide how your new competitor would operate differently to steal your business, try to document what it might take to get a company like this going. What resources would be needed? What infrastructure would be required? What would the employee mix look like? How quickly would they be able to steal your business? How could they offer a parity-or-better product or service than you do now, cheaper than you can?

03. Create a script outlining what they would say to sell against you.

Be brutally honest. Talk about where your business is vulnerable. Ask what potential benefits of this new competitive offering that your customers would respond to that you aren't able to match.

Surprise! You just outlined a business plan.

In those three (obviously multifaceted) steps, you've outlined the product/service design. You've begun to outline a viable financial model. And you've laid the foundation for marketing and sales messaging.

Remember: If you can imagine this, so can a competitor.

With every new technology, it's only disruption when you're the incumbent. For everyone else, it's simply opportunity.

What processes within your business could a competitor improve upon with AI or machine-learning technology?

What resources/buy-in would you need to begin exploring the increased use of machine learning in your business?

Write your competitors' scripts for selling against your new AI infused business experience.

Download a printable PDF of all notes pages at magnani.com/book

DAY 28

Automate as much as possible—but no more.

The robots are coming!

Admittedly, the cliché that the best, fastest and easiest way to be wrong is to try and predict the future, may apply here. That being said, at Magnani, we have been having an increasing level of conversation around the impending impact of AI on the future of business. More specifically, our conversations involved whether AI will change the course of how businesses connect with customers—from that of an artful conversation to an interaction with heartless statistical algorithm. Ultimately, we came to the conclusion that it depends on how much you're willing to embrace technology and how attached you are to the relationships you have with customers today.

Let's follow a few emerging trends and technologies into the future and infer how they're coming together to change the business landscape. And finally, let's explore what businesses can do today to stay ahead and take advantage of the transitions to come.

In the beginning: efficiency and margin for all.

The first AI technologies emerging in the market aren't job killers; they're playing-field levelers and amplifiers. We are already seeing powerful AI tackling jobs and tasks that simply never existed before, because they involve processing and data analysis on a scale that humans simply are not innately capable of handling.

Where we used to approach market segmentation from an intuitive or psychological perspective, now machine-learning algorithms are tackling the job with brute force and an unbiased eye. More customized and personalized user experiences are being driven by better product recommendations fueled by massive cluster analysis.

Google provides these more finely tailored search results using its RankBrain AI. Modern fraud prevention has moved from traditional statistical analysis to incorporating natural-language processing AI to spot suspicious activity. Ad networks rely on AI to behaviorally target ads and optimize cost-per-thousand (CPM) on the fly. And let's not forget the current onslaught of AI-driven, 24-7, low-wage bots handling any number of process-driven customer-service functions, from helping you change an airline reservation to processing payments.

For any business, the advantages come from understanding where the use of current technology can create a more compelling and relevant experience for the customer. Traditionally, we created paths for customers, whether physical or virtual, that were designed to help them navigate a linear process of awareness, understanding, affinity, and purchase. However, the increased prevalence of AI-driven experiences is quickly training customers to expect solutions to be delivered proactively based on what we know and predict about their needs. Remaining competitive today will require user experiences that deliver on that expectation. In simpler terms, we used to create great stores; now, we need to leverage AI to create amazing virtual personal shoppers.

The next advance: coming for the marketers.

If I may paraphrase, the self-comforting statements I hear from many marketers usually go something like, "AI will disrupt media, but machines will never be creative." Even if I subscribed to this prejudice (which I don't), what machines are great at, especially AI-driven machines, is learning rules by example and generating output based on those divined rule sets and measured outcomes. That rule set could easily be as a natural-language creative brief or a set of brand guidelines, or, in more advanced cases, self-defined rules based on machine learning applied to a data set of historically effective advertising. In 2016, Microsoft released a short film about the results of an AI experiment they titled "The Next Rembrandt."

The film documents how, through a process of feeding the complete collection of Rembrandt portraits into a specialized AI, they were able to divine the most common aspects of his works—brush technique, lighting, subject matter, etc.—then have the AI create a "new Rembrandt portrait" from whole cloth, so to speak. The tangible results were astonishing—though arguably neither truly new nor a real Rembrandt.

On the more conceptual side, McCann™ Japan pitted one of its human creative directors against an AI that was fed a diet of award-winning television commercials in a contest to create a new TV spot for Clorets® mints. In the end, consumers preferred the human creative director's work—but advertising professionals found the AI-generated concept to be more creative. Both anecdotes, while impressive, are still one-offs. The true value will be in the ability of AI to generate and iterate thousands of ads for the same product, then optimize deployment around the best-performing. No creative pitch. No rationales. Just measurable results.

And, in early 2019, the research organization Open AI revealed that a machine-learning writing algorithm[29] they had created was too good at its job and might actually present a danger to the public if released without sufficient testing.

So, where does that leave the marketing department? The truth is, as with any automation solution, in most cases, AI creative doesn't have to be better than that produced by the best humans—it only has to be good enough to achieve the desired result at a cost substantially lower than a human. And that means we should expect AI will soon be capable of assuming what I'll call production-level execution.

Commercial applications like thegrid.io are already applying this idea to web design, to mixed but promising results. The real advantage, in the near term, will go to creative agencies that leverage the associative and generative powers of AI as the ultimate brainstorm amplifier. Then apply traditional human curation and execution to the best ideas of the lot—which is exactly what our friends at McCann Japan did, despite their full-on-robot-creative-director PR spin.

[29] https://openai.com/blog/better-language-models/

Infinity and beyond: battle of the bots.

Today, you can have a relatively one-dimensional—though convincingly polite—AI bot named Amy schedule your meetings. Provided by a company called X.ai out of New York, you cc Amy (or, should you choose, Amy's "male" counterpart, Andrew) on any email message where you're attempting to schedule a meeting, and Amy takes over negotiating the date, time, and channel/place. While useful and, admittedly, quite convincing, Amy is a single-purpose AI acting within a highly constrained set of rules. And the math is binary. Either requested slots are available or not, and she fills them accordingly.

You may have encountered Amy already. And, if you ignored the small disclaimer at the bottom of her emails, you could have easily been fooled into becoming jealous of your business acquaintance's ability to hire a personal assistant. But if you had pressed the conversation, Amy would have quickly succumbed to the Turing-test realities of her limited purpose. The more interesting aspect of this technology, however, is what happens when two people who want to schedule a meeting both use Amy. At that point, the emails stop and the two bots "go binary" and negotiate, invisibly, in the background and only alert if a conflict is seemingly unresolvable.

That is a more apt model for imagining how AI will manage our consumer interactions. For businesses, preparing for competing in this inevitable future means developing data-rich user profiles that allow for predictive behavioral modeling and precise segmentation, as well as creating fully abstracted application programming API-level transactions that can easily manifest in voice-, bot-, or human-driven experiences.

Technological progress favors those most adaptable to change.

Someday, marketing might be a hands-off, AI-driven cloud service, as emotionally indifferent as an email server—but not in the near term. As marketers, we shouldn't focus on being replaced by AI, but on being overtaken by human competitors who leverage the technology to connect more meaningfully with our customers.

Perform a SWOT analysis of the state of automation in your business in relation to the industry overall:

Strengths

Weaknesses

Opportunities

Threats

Download a printable PDF of all notes pages at magnani.com/book

DAY
29

Don't outspend them. Outsmart them.

Four ways to be more competitive without spending more.

Whether from disruptive technologies shifting the balance of power, or a proliferation of low-cost competitors gaining access to existing technologies at increasingly lower prices, in every industry, it seems, competition is increasing. In this environment, the importance of being deliberate about how and where you invest time and resources grows exponentially. The "easy" solution, some think, is to increase your budget. But increased budgets without increased focus and strategic consideration are usually simply a recipe for waste. Thankfully, there are a number of "sweat equity" options to help you be more competitive on your existing budget.

01. Audit your competition.

And we mean, actively. Relentlessly. Set time aside and search the web, scour trade publications, visit their social and web properties, and subscribe to their mailing lists. Take screenshots, catalog and document what, when and how they're talking about themselves, your mutual competition, or you. Note when they begin to alter their tone or messaging. Try to understand how they flight media. We, as a species, are incredible pattern-recognition machines. The more you internalize your competitors' behaviors, the more quickly you will anticipate any change to their strategy and the more quickly you can adjust or enhance your own.

02. Narrow your target audience.

This usually feels counterintuitive for most of our clients. Shouldn't you want to sell to more customers? Not exactly. You really want to sell to more of the right customers. Most industries follow something close to the 80/20 rule—meaning, 80% of the profits are derived from the top 20% of customers. By example, let's look at the case of Apple. By dominating in the high end of the mobile market, and ignoring the budget end of the market, they reap something like 90% of the industry profits with only 17% share of unit sales. Evaluate your customer portfolio. Understand the profile of your most profitable relationships and focus your messaging, media mix, and overall marketing budgets against that segment.

03. Upgrade your analytics.

Google Analytics™ lets you track goals based on the basic data that platform can track: URL visited, time on page, or pages per session. With the addition of Google Tag Manager™, you're able to track nearly every type of user interaction on your website. It's a window—not simply into where and how many users are interacting with your site, but also how effectively your site is driving the behaviors that feed your sales funnel or lead to a direct sale itself.

Tag Manager opens up new possibilities of what can be tracked: page timers, video plays, button clicks, form information, window loads, and limitless custom events. And it enables reporting on the event data in Analytics for further detailed analysis down the road. In addition to these being able to trigger Goals in Analytics and Conversions in AdWords, Tag Manager can add the event details to existing reports for maximum slicing and dicing.

04. Optimize your online experience for conversions.

Conversion rate optimization (CRO) is the process of reviewing analytics and user feedback to improve specific performance metrics of your website. That could mean refining web forms to increase completion rates and improve lead generation. It could mean uncovering the most frequent points of exit on your user journey and making adjustments to your UX, your design, the language involved, or adding social appeals to make continuation of the journey more obvious, simple or appealing. In addition to enhancing results on key performance indicators (KPIs), CRO should improve ROI on SEO/SEM efforts as well as create a higher satisfaction rating, sitewide.

Insight and efficiency are always a good investment.

Time and time again, we've seen challenger brands disrupt larger, entrenched incumbents by taking the time and putting in the effort to refine their positioning, narrow their target-customer profile, differentiate their customer experience, and go after their competitors' best customers, relentlessly, with surgical precision. As the French proverb goes: "Qui court deux lievres a la fois, n'en prend aucun"—translation: "Who runs after two hares at the same time, catches none."

Find a whiteboard and fill in a chart like the one below:

	You	Competitor 1	Competitor 2
Positioning			
Main Competitive Advantage			
Key Driver of Success (statistic)			
Key Measure of Success			

What is your optimal conversion metric (e.g., form fill, subscription, sales)?

Looking at your web analytics, what is your current conversion rate?

Looking at your analytics, at what point before a conversion are most visitors abandoning their journey with you?

What could you change about the user experience at the most common point of abandonment to improve conversions by 10%?

Download a printable PDF of all notes pages at magnani.com/book

DAY
30

Keep your chin up.

Yes, you can still get there from here.

Here's the good news: Everyone charged with developing a marketing or business strategy has been there—that point in time and space when you realize the strategy, to which everyone agreed, has not yet delivered satisfactory results—and everyone is looking to you for the fix.

Now, here's the bad news: You feel like you're on your own—and you're probably right.

Thankfully, there are some tried-and-true strategies (besides "polish up the résumé") that have helped even the weariest find their way out of challenging business situations. Here are three strategies, gleaned from the proverbial annals of business, which, depending on your time frame for success, may give you some welcome inspiration for change.

Three strategies every struggling business should think about:

01. Short-term | The Ted Williams strategy: only swing at good pitches.

In his famous book, "The Science of Hitting," baseball great Ted Williams advises would-be players to find and understand their "happy zone." This means that smart, disciplined batters narrow the range of what qualifies as a good pitch—they take fewer swings, but each, theoretically, has a higher chance of success. Translated for marketers, it means several things. From a positioning perspective, it means taking time to review and clarify your positioning.

If you take an honest look at the sum of your efforts and find you're trying to be all things to all people—stop. You're wasting your budget and confusing your market. And, speaking of markets, the Ted Williams strategy applies to customer profiling, too: You should narrow your target market to only those customer segments that show a high willingness to purchase and represent a healthy margin for the business. Among the universe of people you sell to, these segments represent your happy zone. There's little reason to expend precious time, effort, and money on attracting alternative target segments until you've maximized your returns with your core group. From a product-line perspective, it means focusing budget dollars primarily on those products or services that represent the greatest return on marketing (ROM).

Ultimately, this may mean lower unit sales overall and even lower top-line revenues. But it should also mean increased bottom-line profits. Until your promotional efforts have saturated the market for this product or service to the point of diminishing return on investment, it makes little sense to divert budgets elsewhere. Apple applies this strategy in its refusal to manufacture affordable (cheap) iPhones. Inexpensive phones are out of Apple's happy zone, which has proven to be a sage approach, as reflected in its world-leading market cap and it achieving 91% share of the mobile handset industry's profit by 2015[30].

02. Medium-term | The Cortés strategy: making success the only viable option.

In 1519, when Hernán Cortés (de Monroy y Pizarro Altamirano) landed in Veracruz to begin his great conquest (setting aside, for a moment, the disturbing moral implications of said quest), he ordered his men to burn the ships. As the story goes, some of his men thought it was a joke—until they found themselves tipping back a tankard of rum on the beach that evening as the last embers of the bonfire of their way back home smoldered in the twilight. The point of this campfire wasn't to kick off their campaigns in the new world with a party. It was to ensure everyone had no choice left but to focus on the same goal.

Unlike the Ted Williams strategy, which relies strictly on greater focus, the Cortés strategy is about first focusing on the company. This means cutting out products or services that don't meet contribution-margin expectations or do not serve a greater strategic competitive value. The idea is that those underperforming products or services, along with the infrastructure or resources required to support them, are keeping the company from focusing on what will create profitable success.

In the early 2000s, we were privileged to help a company execute this strategy successfully. MacGregor Golf was struggling financially and considering receivership when it asked if we could help resurrect this once-vaunted brand. It was a challenge we couldn't pass up.

By extending the brand from equipment for elite players down to cheap three- and eight-club sets at big-box sporting goods stores, MacGregor had lost relevance among its profitable, high-end target segments, resulting in dramatic declines in sales and market share. We advised exiting these mass-market lines and outlets, and immediately refocusing on delivering only high-end, high-margin products—in effect shrinking the company from nearly $40 million to just over $20 million in annual sales. Combined with a high-profile repositioning of the brand within the trade, we established multiyear communication and tactical strategies for each channel and target. As a result of this restricted product and channel strategy and a re-energized marketing program, MacGregor was able to expand distribution among key green-grass and pro retailers in North America, Europe, and Asia—increasing revenues from $20 million to over $120 million in just four years.

30 http://fortune.com/2016/02/14/apple-mobile-profit-2015/

03. Long-term | The Clayton Christensen strategy: become the unexpected disruptor.

In his seminal work, The "Innovator's Dilemma," Harvard professor Clayton Christensen lays out a compelling landscape where large, successful incumbents become victims of their own success in the face of disruptive technologies. By historic standards, these companies are doing everything right to serve the needs of their customers. But disruptive technology creates an alternative behavior option that can dramatically change or negate the market need those organizations are successfully serving today. So, what is the Clayton Christensen strategy in regard to marketing? Well, as, Xerox PARC Chief Scientist Alan Kay, pioneer of object-oriented programming and the windowing graphical user interface we use on our PCs every day, put it, "The best way to predict the future is to invent it."

This strategy requires taking the perspective that the long-term success of the company depends on seeing your business as a potential disruptor sees it and creating a challenger business model that has the potential to destroy your existing market share before that hypothetical disruptor gains a foothold. In practice, instead of focusing all your products, services, and marketing on maximizing returns from your current market, you should assign part of your budget to investigate and create the next market challenger yourself.

Of course, doing so is certainly not as simple as the length of that last sentence would imply. It requires a commitment to understanding the inner workings of the relationship between your customers and the job your product is being hired to do for them. It means constant, iterative innovation and a venture capitalist's appetite for encountering more dead ends than home runs. And, most important, unlike R&D that is focused on solving a problem five to ten years out, disruptive technologies provide an alternative that can be used today, even at the cost of an existing high-margin business.

IBM successfully built its PC business at the cost of its mainframe business and is currently cannibalizing its mainframe business with cloud services. Netflix killed its own DVD-by-mail business with streaming services. At the start of the first dot-com era, American Airlines created a subsidiary of its Sabre travel agent reservation business and sent it to a separate location with a charge to disrupt the travel-agent business. The result was Travelocity.

The best opportunities are those we create for ourselves.

If history has taught us anything, it should be that business-as-usual delivers results-as-usual. The increasing acceleration of change and technological disruption and complacency hastens risk. The smartest approach is to view our challenges not solely from the historical perspective but from the potentially unflattering perspective of our competitors, our customers, and our potential disruptors.

If you found yourself in a position to require a strategy re-assessment, which of the above might work for you and why? (If none, why not, and what would your alternate strategy look like?)

If you were purchased by a competitor, what changes would they make to your business?

Download a printable PDF of all notes pages at magnani.com/book

See? That didn't hurt a bit.

Unlike the preponderance of business book authors in the world, I actually hope you didn't find any answers in these pages. I do, however, hope you found perhaps a new perspective on how to address a nagging problem. Or a new strategy for innovating new products or services. Or mastered your Swiftian agency interrogation techniques. Or simply learned a few new quotes to use when you toss out your Jack Nicholson impression at parties—yes, I know you have a Jack Nicholson impression. Everyone does.

Watch this space.

Undoubtedly, the pace of change will render one or more of these approaches obsolete, perhaps even before Amazon delivers this volume to your device or doorstep. If so, you can be sure that I will eventually address that particular elephant in the room on my blog, available at the creatively titled URL: magnani.com/blog.

Until then, enjoy the view.

Made in the USA
Columbia, SC
10 February 2020

87593597R30106